TURNING
PASSIONS
INTO
PROFITS

TURNING
PASSIONS
INTO
PROFITS

THREE STEPS TO WEALTH AND POWER

CHRISTOPHER HOWARD

WILEY

John Wiley & Sons, Inc.

Copyright © 2004 by Christopher Howard. All rights reserved.
Published by John Wiley & Sons, Inc., Hoboken, New Jersey.
Published simultaneously in Canada.

Illustrations by Christine Winters, www.theenchanted-castle.com.

For general information on our other products and services please contact our Customer Care Department within the United States at (800) 762-2974, outside the United States at (317) 572-3993 or fax (317) 572-4002.

Wiley also publishes its books in a variety of electronic formats. Some content that appears in print may not be available in electronic books. For more information about Wiley products, visit our web site at www.wiley.com.

Library of Congress Cataloging-in-Publication Data:
Howard, Chris, 1970–
    Turning passions into profits : three steps to wealth and power / Chris Howard.
      p. cm.
    ISBN 0-471-71856-4 (cloth)
    1. Success in business. 2. Entrepreneurship. 3. Creative ability in business. I. Title.
    HF5386.H845 2005
    650.1'2—dc22
2004024102

Printed in the United States of America.

10 9 8 7 6 5

Michael—this one's for you.

Contents

ACKNOWLEDGMENTS

As I say in this book, the best way to carry out any grand vision is by pulling together a great team that helps you take it to that next level and make it happen. *Turning Passions into Profits* is a perfect demonstration of that concept in action. It could not have come together in the time that it did without the dedication and hard work of my fellow teammates.

Big thanks to Karen Corban for being an outstanding partner and friend. I am eternally grateful to Wendy Beacock for being there from the very beginning and for her hard work, support, and advice along the way. To Bob and Cindy Shearin for seeing the spark and fanning the flame. And Helen and Michael Bueno for their unconditional support. I also wish to thank Karen McCreadie for taking a diamond in the rough and turning it into something to be admired; Aricia Lee for making it real in her dedication to the writing process; and, Amy Sorkin for cleaning up our act. I want to acknowledge Chris and Jill Stoten for keeping the machine turning, Christine Winters for her artistry and friendship, Renee Robinson and Joyce Uptmor for all their help along the way, Alexi for his sizzling copywriting, and Deb Korte for having our back.

To the "Dream Team" at The Christopher Howard Companies who help so many make their dreams come true, including my own, here's to an incredible job and an incredible future!

I am also indebted to all of my teachers past and present for allowing me to stand on their tall shoulders so that I could open the doorways to my dreams.

Introduction

Many teachers throughout the years have reminded me of the concept of beginning with the end in mind. In other words, the first step in getting what you want is determining *what* you want. This principle holds a special significance for me as I write the Introduction to this book.

I remember just a few short years ago lying on the bed in my apartment, which was actually just a converted garage, wondering why things were *not* working for me at the time. I was struggling financially. In fact, it got so bad at one point that my gas was cut off and I was bathing with buckets of microwaved water and eating only every third day.

The most frustrating part of it all was the fact that I had read hundreds of books on personal development and had attended seminar after seminar—Tony Robbins, Robert Kiyosaki, Franklin Covey, all of whom I am indebted to for all the great information. Yet I still wasn't able to make my life work. There seemed to be something missing from the equation. I knew what I was supposed to do, but not *how* to do it. I had awakened the giant within, but when I woke him up, he was just as frustrated as I was that we weren't any further along toward fulfillment.

I felt desperately lost and off course. Yet in my heart I knew that I was capable of much more. Perhaps you can relate to the frustration and confusion I was feeling. Have you ever felt like you could have more, be more, or accomplish more in your life, but you just didn't know what was holding you back? Or perhaps you feel you should be further along than you are right now, and you just want to know what it takes to get there. What are the steps?

Well, that's where I was, searching for coins between the couch cushions, when I decided I'd finally had enough. I started to write down huge goals for myself. I wrote furiously for hours. I wrote down all the experiences I wanted to have in my lifetime and all the things I wanted to do. I wrote down all the things I wanted to own, and all the traits and qualities I admired in others. I wrote about my childhood dreams, my ultimate career desires, and the things I had always been passionate about. I didn't let any judgments enter my head. I just wrote down everything that I wanted to be, do and have in my life, no matter how ridiculous it seemed at the time. I didn't worry about *how* it was going to happen. I just committed myself to gaining clarity on exactly *what* I wanted to create.

Many of my goals seemed impossibly out of reach at the time based on my circumstances. I was following my true passions, but I was still very broke. Little did I know that I was unleashing the passion and potential that would end up paving the way toward the entirely new way of life I now enjoy. Take a look at these five examples:

1. I wrote that I would be speaking around the country at some point in my life. I now conduct seminars and training programs on wealth, leadership, and personal influence for thousands of people around the world.
2. I wrote that I would have a high-rise office on the ocean. As I write this, I'm gazing out my window at a school of dolphins jumping in the water, so close that it looks like I could reach out and touch them!
3. I wrote that I would be on a career path I really enjoyed. Today I get to help people break through their greatest challenges and transform their lives. I find this work exciting and motivating, and I know I'm blessed to feel so passionate about my life's work.
4. I wrote that I would be making every day an epic adventure and living life to the max. Whether I am leading one of my seminar groups, hang-gliding, or hot-air ballooning over the beautiful resort town of Palm Springs, I am truly living life to the fullest—and I get to assist others to do the same, which is one of my greatest sources of joy.
5. I wrote that I would become a multimillionaire. I've since gone from $70,000 in debt to making $2 million in two and a half

years. In that same time, I went from living in a ghetto to living in a house on a cliff overlooking the ocean. My income continues to double and triple beyond my expectations. I have now set my sights on billions, which I am currently building. At this point, I don't do it for the money as much as for the fun and challenge. I plan to give my personal wealth back to society at the end of my life in the form of a charitable foundation.

Most of the goals that I wrote down on that red-letter day in the little converted garage have come true. I say this not to impress you, but rather to impress upon you what you, too, are capable of. How did I do it? By applying the techniques presented in this book, including a system I developed called Cognitive Reimprinting™ for replicating the success traits and strategies of others.

First, in the process of filling those notebooks, I discovered what I actually *believed* to be true, as opposed to all that I wished to be true in my life. I woke up to my own small version of reality. I realized I had a long-held belief that either you do what you are passionate about *or* you go out and make money. I had been living part of my passion, traveling all over the world, but finances were still my biggest challenge. The mental block was that I considered myself one of those people who follows his heart. In my mind at the time, I thought that making money required "selling out" or becoming "a suit." Since I perceived passion and profit to be mutually exclusive, I was proving the dichotomy true in my experience. This limiting belief was just one aspect of my personality that was preventing me from also being someone who creates wealth and fulfillment on a large scale. I was opening my eyes to how my perceptions were literally shaping my world.

Next, my immense frustration and pain over my situation drove me to begin intensive study of the people whom I admired most—world leaders like Martin Luther King Jr., Mahatma Ghandi, and Nelson Mandela, and legends of the business world like Richard Branson, founder of the Virgin empire; billionaire investor Warren Buffett; and famed billionaire entrepreneur Oprah Winfrey—to figure out what made them tick. What set them apart from the rest of us? What I discovered, ironically enough, is that the people who create massive wealth and achieve unprecedented success are those people who are truly passionate about what they do. As Donald Trump's father told his son before he became a world-renowned billionaire real estate developer, "If you're not passionate about what you do, you'll never stick with it long enough to truly become successful." From all I was learning, it was becoming very obvious to me that I was the only thing holding me back from pursuing both my passion and profit. The good news was that meant I had the ultimate control over making my own success. This got me very excited and extremely motivated.

I continued to actively research great leaders, thinkers, and achievers in every field to find an alternative route that I would feel more deeply passionate about. Earlier in my career I had worked with several leadership and communication companies, soaking up new knowledge, skills, and information. I had sought out the best technologies for accelerated behavioral change available, and found the cutting-edge tools of Ericksonian hypnosis and Neuro Linguistic Programming (NLP) to be the best of the best at that time. I believed in these tools so much that I became a seminar leader, traveling the world teaching these life-changing therapeutic techniques and communication tools. Both sciences were highly effective for assisting people to make rapid and lasting behavioral change.

However, I soon realized that getting rid of, or changing, the behaviors I no longer wished to experience in my life was only part of the success puzzle. After getting clear about what I wanted to create instead, and how I was going to create it, I needed to do it quickly. I didn't want to take another 10 years to make my life the way I wanted it. In this fast-paced culture, time was a valuable asset I didn't have. A business venture had left me $70,000 in debt. I was determined to turn my life around immediately. Reading and studying took a lot of time, and no one paid me for it. Predominant characteristics, mind-sets, strategies, habits, attitudes, and thought patterns were emerging from my in-depth research of billionaires and world leaders. I knew from all my earlier experience that NLP's effectiveness came from modeling behavioral change. Therefore, I was sure that by modeling ultimate success, I could train my own mind and install habits that would allow me to replicate the results of the most powerful leaders in the world. But I had to understand every aspect of their mind-sets first. That's when I developed a system called Cognitive Reimprinting™. From detailed cognitive profiles and mind maps of all my own role models and their hidden internal filters, I rapidly installed their attitudes, mind-sets, behaviors, and strategies in myself in order to replicate their effective success patterns in my own life. Then I used my newfound knowledge and skills to catapult myself forward in my career and my life to the level of passion and profit I enjoy today.

The great news is that I have distilled the very best of my research and techniques into a system that works as a software for the mind, upgrading its functioning to achieve results faster than ever. And I am presenting this comprehensive system here for the first time in this book as Creation Technologies™. It's the entire set of techniques for rapidly re-creating your life the way you want it. No matter what the picture of success looks like to you, within these pages is a template for making that dream a reality. I like to think of *Turning Passions into Profits* as the art and science of achieving results, incorporating everything I have used to live out my grandest ambitions and boldest dreams thus far. Consider this book a toolbox full of tools and techniques for building the ultimate vision of your life, complete with an instruction manual for the mind and the software to download the mind-set of success.

You will learn step-by-step how to not only get inside the heads of the world's most accomplished leaders, but how to emulate their dazzling results more rapidly and efficiently than believed possible. If you no longer feel passionate about life, if you're not sure what your purpose is, if you feel the need for some major change but are not sure where to start, you are starting in the right place. I guarantee that if you read this book and *apply* the technologies that lie within, *you will change your life.* You will have the power to rapidly close the gap between where you are and where you want to be. And that's a promise.

Creation Technologies™

Sir Isaac Newton once said, "The reason I see so far is because I stand on the tall shoulders of those who came before me."

I have certainly stood on the tall shoulders of those that have come before me in the writing of this book and the development of Creation Technologies™. Many of the diverse ideas and concepts combined and presented here have been adapted from the multitude of teachers on my journey. Many of the tools are also of my own making. I have combined them all under the umbrella I call Creation Technologies™—a specific set

of techniques that (1) expands your perception of the world and your experience in it to increase what is possible, and (2) empowers you to cause your
future, rather than let it be merely an effect of the past and everyone else.

Often, groundbreaking discoveries are the result of bringing together ideas that previously seemed unrelated. For example, Newton's
law of universal gravitation was theorized by relating, for the first time,
the gravitational pull of planets to objects' weight on Earth. We have
long since accepted the connection between the mind's thought patterns
and success. Many books have even been written on the subject. Perhaps
the most famous of these is *Think and Grow Rich*, written in 1960 and
still considered a classic self-improvement text to this day. Its author,
Napoleon Hill, dedicated his life to studying and learning from successful people. *Think and Grow Rich* spawned a tidal wave of similar books
over the years, many of them excellent. *Turning Passions into Profits* is the
modern version of *Think and Grow Rich* with the added power of today's
most innovative technologies and advanced knowledge of the brain's ca-
pacities. Although I bring to light subjects ranging from quantum
physics to the way the brain processes information to the power of
metaphors, I assure you that they are all related to building wealth and
personal power. If you experience any confusion while taking in the full
scope of information presented, realize that a state of confusion always
precedes deeper understanding. As you stay with the processes, you will
be amazed at the bigger picture that emerges of your life's possibilities,
your own power to plot its course, and how you can find yourself arriving at your chosen destination quicker than you ever imagined.

There are several books on business and personal finances available
these days. There are also plenty out there on self-development. Yet I
typically meet thousands of people through my work who, despite reading these books, cannot apply the information to their own lives.

Why not?

I believe it is because *success* doesn't mean the same thing to everybody. You can find information on smart investing, real estate, flipping
properties, managing, getting out of debt, staying motivated, even money
as energy. However, each of us is playing a different game from a different
vantage point. Not everyone is starting from the same place. If you wanted
to go to Los Angeles, for example, directions to get there would vary depending on whether you were in Washington, D.C., or in Australia.

What *is* possible is to describe the governing principles of success, wealth, and power that apply to any desired outcome. For me, *success* means being in a position where I can positively impact people's lives. My definition of *wealth* is living a life of abundance in every area, from financial resources to happiness and fulfillment of purpose. *Power* is the ability to effectively produce results in whatever area I choose. This is what I call being a magician of the material world, creating spectacular results seemingly out of nothing. For you it may be different. Personal clients and participants in my seminars have used these principles and techniques with successful results in every field, whether they were looking to get more clients; start a new business; increase their company's net worth; be an effective parent; achieve greater health; create stronger relationships; or be a powerful trainer, successful actor, or persuasive politician.

To turn your passions into profits, you must first wake up to the internal rules you are currently playing by and expand your field of possibilities. Where are you now? Where exactly do you want to go? Step 1 is understanding the science and neurology behind how your mind is currently determining what is possible for you and what is out of reach.

Oliver Wendell Holmes once said, "A mind that is stretched to a new idea never returns to its original dimensions." Some of the ideas presented here may seem alien to you at first; some may be familiar. Some may, as Holmes suggests, stretch your mind so it will never return to its original dimensions. Just keep in mind that even if a belief cannot be proven true or false, it can be proven effective or ineffective. In other words, if your particular view of the world is not empowering, you can choose one that is. That is the basis and purpose of the tools presented in this book, including Neurological Repatterning™.

Cognitive Reimprinting™ (CR)

Step 2 then is to find and study your personal role models, those individuals who have already produced results in those areas in which you want to succeed. This is done using genius reading, mind mapping, and cognitive profiling, all techniques to maximize your brain's power and utilize others' life lessons for faster transformation. The mind is literally able to alter existing thought patterns and behaviors to those that are more effective in accomplishing specific outcomes. Step 2 goes into detail about what particular thought processes and behavioral patterns of billionaires and other masters of their game make them so extremely successful. You will learn how to create a cognitive profile based on their personalities, then install within your own personality those necessary strategies, traits, habits, beliefs, and skill sets you choose from your role models to embody your fullest potential. That is Cognitive Reimprinting™.

I uncovered several common ingredients among billionaires and world leaders, and I go into much greater detail about these in Step 2. One of the prevalent attitudes I found was that most of these billionaires considered wealth building a kind of game. Richard Branson doesn't even make the commonly accepted distinction between work and play. As he said in his interview with *Fortune* magazine, "I don't think of work as work and play as play. It's all living." That is why I chose the metaphor of the playing field of life, choosing your game, and playing to win. It's an extremely empowered perspective compared to the long-held "work for the man, play after retirement" standard. The game of life is also a powerful analogy to explain the complexities of Creation Technologies™ in a way that is easier to understand. Consequently, I use these terms to convey the principles of leadership, communication, and the mind's relationship to producing results. *Success* in general is playing the game of life on your own terms. This, I believe, ultimately comes down to listening to your heart's desire—your passion.

However, sometimes it's not enough to do what you love and just wait for the money to follow. No matter what field you choose to excel in, like any athlete on a playing field, you need to get proficient at a specific set of skills, maintain focus on your ultimate purpose, and know how to consistently hit goal after goal. Each of us plays a different game on a different playing field with different teammates. All of those factors govern the final outcome—whether you win.

You will create your own picture of what winning will look like to you. Every legend of wealth and power has his or her own mentors. Bill Gates read everything he could on Napoleon. Oprah modeled Phil Donahue and Barbara Walters. Athletes study tapes of their own performances and watch closely other masters of their game. Step 2 is to find the masters who have gone before you and follow their lead. Learn from their accomplishments and failures. Download and install any aspect of their success you choose. As you come across new experiences in your growing success, you will have their resources and reference points to draw from in any new situation or challenge.

Walt Disney once said, "You can have the most beautiful dream in the world, but it takes people to build it." That has certainly been true for multibillionaire Richard Branson, who could not have created his Virgin empire alone. He created it with and through other people. The ability to create strategic partnerships and synergistic relationships is essential to your success. Those who produce extraordinary results, from Gandhi to Gates, are those who used their ability to get groups of people working together toward a common objective.

Step 3 outlines the skill sets necessary to master the art of communication and leadership. Here is where your passion will prove essential. Like any team sport, your game cannot be played and won alone. You cannot win a game of soccer with just a goalkeeper. You need to engage the whole team in a powerful symbiosis. Leadership goes beyond management in that it is the ability to inspire others in a way that gets them excited to work together toward a shared vision. The larger the vision, the greater the need to convey that grand vision in such a way that others want to join you in achieving it.

This last section focuses specifically on learning the set of techniques that great leaders use to harness others' power and talents to create win-win solutions for everyone. If everyone is excited about producing the same outcome and the objective is fulfilling for all, then the whole team marches confidently in the direction of the shared dreams. Obviously, Martin Luther King Jr. was an absolute master at this art of communication and leadership. But *how*, specifically, did he arouse such inspiration and motivation in others? Whether in the business, political, or personal arena, all great leaders possess the essential qualities of character and set of skills described in Step 3. The exercises there will enable you to formulate your own ultimate mission and vision, and then think, speak, negotiate, and sell to create a team that will ultimately carry your vision forward.

I'm thrilled to have the opportunity to share this knowledge and experience with you, and I hope to meet you at some point in the future on your journey to living the life you deserve!

STEP

Wake Up!

CHAPTER

Wake Up to Possibility!

*We are boxed in by the boundary
conditions of our thinking.*

—Albert Einstein

The New World

Before it was proven that the world was round, it was a well-known "fact" that it was flat. This "fact" was so widely accepted that no one dared test it, because they thought if they did sail out beyond the horizon they would fall off the edge. In other words, because they believed it couldn't be done, it wasn't done.

That is, until Christopher Columbus questioned common knowledge and asked "What if?" That question literally expanded the boundaries of his country, changed history, and permanently altered accepted reality forever.

In spite of our tendency to think of reality as the nonnegotiable basis of our experience, the definition of *reality* changes every time someone pushes the boundary conditions of conventional wisdom. When our perception of reality changes, our behavior changes accordingly, based on what is newly considered possible. When Columbus returned from

3

the New World, a revised world map was drawn up and this began a new era of exploration and adventure. Of course, this had always been possible, but until Columbus proved it by actually sailing over the horizon and managing to return, people's thinking limited how far they dared to venture and what they dared to attempt.

Examples of the impossible being made possible can be found throughout history. When Chuck Yeager flew the X-1, he shattered the myth that there was such a thing as a sound barrier. His training and instincts, combined with the new technology of the day, not only enabled him to go beyond the speed of sound, but reinforced the fact that even alleged technological barriers can be overcome. And what about Roger Bannister? On May 6, 1954, he became the fastest man on the planet when he ran a mile in 3 minutes, 59.4 seconds. The closest anyone had come prior to this was 4 minutes 01.4 seconds in 1945. By breaking the 4-minute mile, a feat previously thought to be humanly impossible, Bannister broke through what Einstein referred to as "the boundary conditions of our thinking." Bannister said at the time, "Now that I have broken the four-minute mile it will be done again—it is like breaking the sound barrier of sport." And he was right—as soon as it was proven possible, many others followed suit and the new record was soon broken.

The self-development tools within this book allow you to break through your own boundary conditions of what you believe is possible in your life, duplicate the success of others you choose to model, then improve upon their success to make it your own.

People often approach me in my seminars with statements such as, "I can't make money. I never had it growing up," or, "I'll never be successful because my parents never supported me," "I don't have the right education to create wealth," or "I can't pursue my dreams because I have too many obligations." I even hear, "I can't do what I want in my life because I don't have the money." Each one of these individuals is living an illusion. These statements are clear indicators of the boundary conditions of their own thinking. They are accepting certain seeming truths about themselves that are then proven true by their experience. They are coming up against their own individual horizons beyond which they cannot conceive of venturing. Yet they are sure that they are doing battle with external obstacles over which they have little or no control. What many people do not yet realize is that these obstacles are just part of the illusion they are creating internally. They have the power to prove *anything* true that they believe and perceive, including more positive outcomes.

Success follows beliefs such as, "I have all I need to be incredibly wealthy and massively successful." Warren Buffett, the most successful investor of all time, was once asked, "How have things changed for you now that you have incredible wealth?" He responded, "Well, I can afford anything I want . . ." Then he paused before adding, ". . . but then again, I always could." Even before Buffett had actually created the wealth he enjoys today, he already had the mind-set of wealth—and therefore the power to create it, because he saw the world in those terms. "The reasonable man adapts himself to the world," wrote George Bernard Shaw, "the unreasonable one persists in trying to adapt the world to himself. Therefore all progress depends on the unreasonable man." When we dare to go beyond our own internal boundary conditions, we discover a whole new world of possible futures for ourselves.

Let's play a little game . . .

It's called the "What's Possible" game. The dictionary definition of *possible* is something "that can or may be, exist, happen, or be done." So for each of the following questions I want you to answer yes or no. Has someone, somewhere on the planet today, achieved these things?

- Is it possible to have a million dollars in the bank?
- Is it possible to have a successful business?
- Is it possible to wake up excited about life?
- Is it possible to have happy, loving relationships?
- Is it possible to be fit and healthy?
- Is it possible to find your life's work and feel passionate about your life most of the time?
- Is it possible to jump off a tall building and fly?

Apart from the last question (and please don't test the theory), all of the above are possible.

Do you agree?

You will no doubt have experienced one of the side effects of this game as you answered the questions. This is called the "yes, buts." The "yes, buts" are responses such as "Yes, but that won't happen to me," or "Yes, but that's because they had privileges I don't have," and so forth.

These pesky little side effects come from the little voice in your head. If you're wondering what the little voice is, it's the voice that just said, "What little voice?"

Ignore the "yes, buts" for the time being. All I want you to do right now is open your mind to the possibility that the world is made up of a countless array of experiences from the very worst to the very best. I want you to get your head around the idea and feel comfortable that everything is possible. You may not agree with this at the moment, but over the next few chapters I will attempt to prove this to you. I say "attempt to" because at the end of the day, whether you decide to believe it is out of my control. All I can do is present the evidence and ask you to draw your own conclusions. For now I ask that you just allow the idea that all things are possible to exist in your mind.

As someone once said, "A mind is like a parachute—it works best when open." This book is an exploration of the mind. What better way to begin than by prying it open? And here is my promise: If you open your mind as you read this book from start to finish and implement the techniques, you will enjoy a more abundant and fulfilling life. If you find it doesn't serve you, you can slam it shut again—the book and your mind.

CHAPTER 2

The Playing Field of Life

For things to change, we must change.
—Henry David Thoreau

So if all things are possible, what is it that dictates what is possible *for you*? Logic would say that the only difference between what is possible and what you experience is *you*.

Figure 2.1 illustrates this point. On the left you have "The Playing Field of Pure Potentiality." This sphere represents the infinite possibilities in the world—wealth, poverty, great relationships, optimum physical health, disease, depression, happiness, basically everything—everything that is possible, everything that anyone at some point in history has experienced, or someone in the future will experience.

On the right is "You." This sphere represents what you experience in your world. You are the creator of your own world. You are the one who decides what and who becomes a part of it. How much you experience and what you experience are determined only to the extent that you allow yourself to expand and move into life by encompassing more of the Playing Field of Pure Potentiality. (See Figure 2.2.)

The overlap where "You" meet infinite possibility is your unique

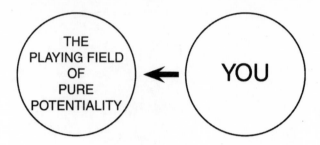

Figure 2.1   The Playing Field and You

"Game." This represents your current experiences. What game are you experiencing? Are you happy? Do you experience abundance and power or poverty? Do you feel like a winner or a loser? Are you experiencing fulfilling relationships? Do you want to be?

In later chapters, I will explain why it is that you experience what you experience. Remember Einstein's quote at the start of the book: "We are boxed in by the boundary conditions of our thinking." Basically, the size, shape, and color of our experience are limited only by the boundaries we put on our thinking, over which we don't let ourselves cross. The boundary you impose on what is possible for you is illustrated in Figure 2.3.

An invisible wall limits what we experience. Everyone has heard the expression "hitting a brick wall"—habitual thought patterns make

Figure 2.2   Your Current Game

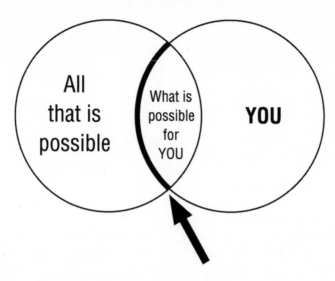

Figure 2.3 Boundary Conditions of *Your* Thinking

up this brick wall! You may have experienced doing something and then standing back from your action and wondering, "Why did I do that?" Or you may have repeated a bad choice over and over again and been perplexed at why. Most of us have experienced that confusion or frustration as to why we continue to do the things we do, even when sometimes we know they are not good for us. These are the invisible boundaries at work. The good news is that there are tools to become aware of them and demolish those that don't serve your best interest so that you can make different choices and experience more of what you want and less or none of what you don't want.

Without those tools, our experience of life—the game we play—can be rather small. And so your playing field may look more like the overlap in Figure 2.4.

With the tools and knowledge presented in this book, you can expand your experience of life so that the game you are playing will look like the one depicted in Figure 2.5.

Just think about it for a second. We each live in our own world. Take for example the contrasting worlds of a bodybuilder, a businessman, and a Fijian fisherman.

The professional bodybuilder wakes up early in the morning and

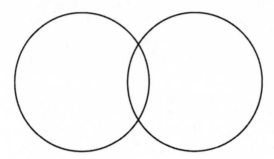

Figure 2.4 Limited Game

heads to the gym. He spends his day planning meals and working his muscles to exhaustion. His life is centered on the upcoming competition for which he has been training zealously over the past several months.

What about the world of a business tycoon? His life is all about the latest deal. He is riding in the back of his limousine reading over the financial statement of a new business in which he is considering investing. He is being driven to the airport where he will board his private jet in order to head out to an important meeting concerning the merger of his company; the merger will soon be made public.

Then there's the Fijian fisherman—he wakes up early in the morning and casts his nets out into the ocean. His days are spent catching and cleaning fish and then taking them to the market to sell. In the

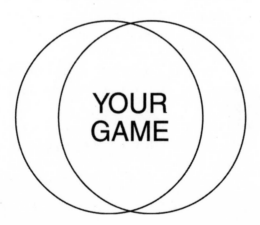

Figure 2.5 Expanded Experience of Life

evening he relaxes, sitting on the dock, drinking a cold beer, and watching the sunset.

Very different playing fields—very different games, as shown in Figure 2.6.

The primary difference between these experiences is their choices. Their external worlds are nothing but reflections of their internal values, beliefs, attitudes, and the other major filters to their experience. These come together to form the boundary conditions of their thinking, which in turn create a different reality for each one.

There is nothing to stop the fisherman from deciding to learn about the stock market and trade online from his oceanside cabin. There is nothing to stop the businessman from hiring a personal trainer and dedicating himself to working out. There is nothing to stop the bodybuilder from giving it all up and becoming a fisherman on a tropical island—nothing, that is, except the boundary conditions of their thinking, which determines their chosen focus.

If you don't already have all the things you wish to be, do, or have, you can learn to reprogram your unconscious mind to work in total con-

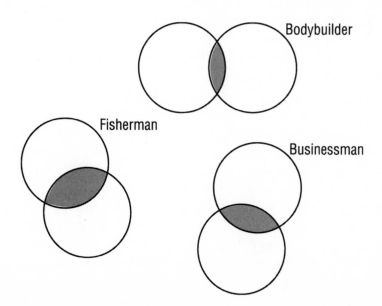

Figure 2.6   A Unique Game for Each Person

gruence with your conscious mind to create it all. That is the game of life. Most of us are walking around in a trance of disempowerment, so wrapped up in our worries, fears, and doubts, and reacting to outer circumstances, that we miss most of the beauty and potential around and within us. It's time to wake up and learn to use all the creative power we have at our fingertips.

You wouldn't have bought this book if you didn't know that you have more potential than you currently exhibit. Perhaps you find yourself in a position that doesn't fulfill much or any of your highest desires. Perhaps you are playing too small. Once you fully wake up from the "You" you've defined yourself to be, you will be able to fully engage in your game of life and go for it. Or you may choose a new one to encompass more of the dreams that lie beyond what you currently think is possible.

Take Oprah Winfrey, for example. If she had not expanded her view of the world as a child by reading books, she would never have risen from the poverty and hardship of her early life to where she is now. Oprah is a master of constantly expanding her playing field and taking others with her. The way she started was by seeking out possibilities. As she tells it, "When I was a young girl growing up in Mississippi, I would have never known that anything existed other than the poverty I lived in if it weren't for the books I read." Reading all those books expanded her references, her self-concept, and, therefore, her playing field of potentiality. By doing this she transformed her own reality to play a much bigger game on a global scale, and influenced us all along the way.

You may think you are limited. You are not limited. Your personal power expands and contracts according to your thinking. Whatever business or relationship you are in, you can literally expand your potential, your skills, and your abilities at any time as you expand your perceptions of what is possible. Anything you desire that currently seems to you beyond your reach or outside your realm of possibility is only so because it lies just outside the boundary conditions of your thinking in this moment. Your thinking, and therefore what you can achieve, can change in an instant. When Bill Gates was growing up, he read every book on Napoleon Bonaparte he could find. This stimulated his imagination, expanded what he felt was possible, and thereby changed the world.

Perhaps you are not making the kind of money you feel you deserve and would like to learn to be truly wealthy. Perhaps you feel you are all alone and would like to include phenomenal relationships in your experience. One of the best ways to take charge of the game you're playing is to understand yourself better; expand your references by modeling excellence from people that have already achieved the type of success you admire; then apply their strategies to your own life. You will exponentially speed up your journey from where you are now to where you want to be.

The size of the game you choose to play is as much up to you as is the game itself. You may choose whatever you want. One is no better than another. The size of the game is dependent only on the amount of knowledge you are willing to gain. You can be, do, have, and create anything you want in life. By increasing your knowledge and understanding of yourself, the true nature of the world, and what power is, you automatically increase the size of the game. That is to say, you widen the playing field that you can play upon. That means greater opportunity to create what you want.

CHAPTER 3

Focus

You think me a child of circumstances.
I make my circumstances.

—Ralph Waldo Emerson

As far back as the 1800s, William James, the father of American psychology, was quoted as saying, "Focus is everything. If only we had a way to teach it, that would be an education extraordinaire! But it seems to be too difficult to teach." Well, times have changed. I teach thousands of people all over the world in my seminars this "education extraordinaire." I have gathered and developed the most cutting-edge tools to date for taking charge of your focus, and thereby taking charge of your life.

Have you ever wondered what separates highly successful people from the rest of the pack? Take multibillionaire Richard Branson, CEO of the Virgin group of companies, for example. Here's a guy who has produced massive results in terms of net worth and he seems to attract teams of people who love working for him. Have you ever wondered what makes Branson, Branson? Or what creates a humanitarian such as Mahatma Gandhi, who transformed the face of a nation? Ever wondered what it was that made him take a stand and create change in the country when no one else would? Clearly he didn't do that alone—he couldn't have. Instead, he mobilized a country to make change without violence by inspiring others with his vision of how the world could be different. What was it that made him step up as the leader to accomplish those things? Or look at Oprah Winfrey. Have you ever wondered what makes Oprah, Oprah? She was able to create the number one talk show in television history and became a billionaire with an international media empire, yet she came from a background of poverty. How is that possible?

What makes these people different? What separates them from the rest of the crowd? Those questions are what drove me to develop Creation Technologies™. I had been to all the seminars and read all the books, but there were still many facets of my life that weren't working, and I was frustrated. I had seen others who had done the seminars too, and although their thinking had shifted on certain levels and things were better in some ways, they still were not able to translate that information and make things happen on a level that I knew they were capable of—and that I knew *I* was capable of.

So I started to pore over biography after biography, in an attempt to find out what was unique about our leaders. We can research movements, thoughts, and ideas until the end of our days, but the true answers to how to create wealth and power lie in the very people who created it themselves. The keys lie within those individuals who possessed whatever special combination of traits, thoughts, values, and behaviors it takes to inspire a humanitarian uprising, head a corporate empire, or lead a nation.

So I studied those people who moved the world in magical ways and I asked what it was that made the difference. Creation Technologies™ is the result of those years of research. The more I researched, the more I realized that there were some fundamental characteristics, attitudes, tools, and strategies that made these people stand out. And the really exciting thing about this discovery was that there are common characteristics and all of them are duplicable. Sometimes when we look at those we admire we place them on an unreachable pedestal and assume they are so far away from who we are that their achievements would be impossible for us to attain. It's a common false belief that those "stars" who stand out in history were either born into wealth or were special in some way—in other words, not like the rest of us. What I found is that this is simply not true.

There are steps to greatness. Branson didn't suddenly wake up one day a multibillionaire. Oprah didn't suddenly realize she was one of the most influential people in America overnight. There is a strategy, a process, and some foundational characteristics that are prevalent in brilliance. Learn those and you can replicate any type of success you choose. First, however, you must clear space in your own mind for the new behaviors by discovering what makes you tick, what beliefs, attitudes, and habits could be determining your life's circumstances.

What You Focus On Determines Your Reality

Earlier this year I had the good fortune of being invited by Berkshire-Hathaway, Warren Buffett's company, to its annual shareholders' meeting, although I am not currently a shareholder. When Buffett first purchased the company, its stock was trading at $12 to $18 a share. At this writing, it's reached $100,000 a share and climbing, making Buffett the second richest man in the world. When someone at the meeting asked him, "What do you attribute your success to?" Buffett responded with a story.

He said that when Bobby Fisher, the American chess player, was playing chess against a Russian player, a big debate ensued about whether a human being could beat a computer at chess. All the articles coming out on the question were saying that a human being would never be able to beat a computer because a computer could think through every infinitesimal possibility and choose the best move to win the game. But what they found was just the opposite—a human being could not only tie the computer, but could sometimes even beat it through a process of what Buffett called "selective grouping." Selective grouping is the internal process by which humans can automatically discount 90 percent of possibilities without ever having to consider them fully, so that they can focus their attention on the remaining 10 percent of possible moves that would make the greatest strategic impact. "If you want to know what makes our overwhelming success," Buffett responded, "It's been selective grouping. It's what we *focus* on. And equally important, it's what we choose not to focus on."

The process of choosing what to focus on is occurring in your brain every second of every day. And it is determining what you experience in your life and what you don't experience. It's a great lesson to apply to time management. It also speaks volumes about focus as one of the most important factors in producing results, since you cannot experience that which you don't put your attention on.

There are two forces at work that govern what you experience. They are inextricably linked, and this chapter is dedicated to the first of those—focus. Your world takes on the form that you recognize only after it has passed through your perceptual filters. It's very important to realize that what information is processed and what information is missed depends completely on the individual. For example, isn't it possible that the business tycoon may never notice the billboard for the men's bodybuilding competition? Wouldn't you admit that the Fijian fisherman might totally miss an announcement in the financial pages of the business merger? And the professional bodybuilder is less likely than the fisherman to get excited about today's tides. These things are not important to them, and therefore may never appear in their reality.

The *only* thing that determines your concept of reality, the *essential* thing that differs between you and someone achieving what you want to achieve is what you choose to concentrate your focus on versus what they are focusing on. Your focus creates what is real for you in your world. I will show you how you can actually change your experiences by changing your focus.

In the book *Chaos*, author James Gleick says that the human nervous system is designed to impose order on a chaotic universe. All around you is a "quantum soup" of atoms and molecules that are constantly shifting and changing. You create your reality by tuning in to and translating certain frequencies that take shape through your perceptions and create what you know as reality. Whether consciously or not, in a quantum universe you choose what to look for and what you experience. Here is a profoundly moving example of focus, or intention, in action.

In the book *Man's Search for Meaning*, Viktor Frankl described his experience as a prisoner in four different Nazi death camps in Germany during World War II. Most of his immediate family died in the camps, including his parents, his brother, and his wife. Dr. Frankl, a neurologist and psychiatrist, examined in his book the difference between those who pushed on to survive, and those who gave in to circumstance and withered away, or died in defeat.

The major difference, he said, was that those who lived focused on a different outcome. They found a way to ascribe a grander purpose or meaning to their current circumstances and existence. By doing this, these people, who were living in the most unimaginably difficult conditions, found a larger vision and saw their current circumstances as being just the thing that would allow them to accomplish that larger vision. Perhaps, they thought, their experience there would allow them to teach the world about the horrors of the holocaust, and thereby be a catalyst to end such terrible atrocities in the world forever. It was this different focus and larger vision that literally kept them alive.

The amazing thing is, whether that belief was true or not is irrelevant. Having it was what made the difference in their outcome. By believing something good would come from their experience, they were able to survive. So, whether something good did actually come from their experience was not important in the end—they survived! Your focus creates what is real for you in your world. By changing your focus you can actually change your experiences. As was proved by Dr. Frankl and many others, focus can literally save your life.

Here is another important concept. You can have whatever you want in life to the extent that you are willing to pay—and what you have to pay is attention.

I am going to explore this concept more fully, including from a quantum physics perspective, but before I do, I want you to really get the concept that your reality is dependent on your focus. One of the best and most powerful ways to do that is through experience. What I want you to do is very simple and will take two minutes. Read all the instructions before you start the exercise:

Have a look around the room or area that you are in right now. I want you to notice as many things as possible that are blue. Don't write them down. Just take a few moments to notice all the things around you that are blue.

When you are satisfied that you have found as many blue things as possible, I want you to close your eyes and count out on your fingers all of the different objects or things that you remember being blue. No peeking!

Once you have finished, make a mental note of how many things you came up with.

Ready . . . go!

Open your eyes. Now flick forward to the end of this chapter and read the question at the bottom of the last page. After you've read the question, close your eyes immediately again—*do not look around*—and answer the question at the end of this chapter. You will count how many things you can remember and make another mental note of that figure.

Okay, go!

Obviously this is slightly more difficult to do in a book than in a live presentation, because even if you didn't peek, your peripheral vision may have caught a few objects, once the second question was raised in your mind. However, my guess is that you will have found significantly more blue objects than objects that fit the question at the end of this chapter.

So the question is, why did you find more blue objects? The answer is simple—you were looking for blue objects. It was your focus and intention to find blue objects, so that's exactly what you did.

The same thing happens in life. The important question to consider now is, what is it that you are truly spending your time focusing on in the world? The things you want or those things you don't want? By working that out, you can choose to focus on other things in order to have other experiences.

This is such a powerful concept on its own that it can have a massive impact in your life. It certainly did for a woman who attended one of my trainings. She approached me and mentioned that she was having severe financial problems, yet she desperately wanted to realize her dream of starting a business to help troubled teenagers. I explained to her that there are 13 trillion dollars circulating the planet each and every day and that this is a totally abundant universe. There are people out there who are literally giving money away, money that she could use to get her business started. She called me two weeks later and said that she had found tens of thousands of dollars available in grant money to launch her new company. The money had always been there—she simply had to change her focus in order to pull it into her experience, and by doing so she instantaneously changed her world.

This woman had had a set view of what was possible, and those boundary conditions limited her from expanding her field of vision to see what else was out there. Changing her focus changed everything.

The Map Is Not the Territory

In 1933, in the book *Science and Sanity*, linguist Alfred Korzybski said, "The map is not the territory." What he meant is that your internal representations, thoughts, or internal "maps" are not reality itself. Think about it—the best map of California can never *be* California. Even if it were built to scale and perfectly designed, it still wouldn't be California. Much in the same way, the thoughts that you have about what is happening outside of you can never *be* what is really outside of you.

Your map is only a representation of the external circumstances. For example in the movie *The Great Outdoors*, John Candy and Dan Aykroyd are looking out at a forest landscape. While Candy's character says, "I look out and I see a beautiful forest with rich natural resources," Aykroyd replies, "I look out and I see construction, buildings, and free enterprise." They are both looking at the same thing, but what they see is very different based on their individual models of the world. When Donald Trump passes by a building in New York, he sees something entirely different than does the person selling coffee on the street corner. Most of us think that our own perceptions of reality are the truth, but truth is subjective.

Reality is subject to the expectations of the individual. That means that we do not just have to cope with our circumstances, as is so often our experience. Our circumstances adapt to our expectations. That is why we don't always get what we want, but we do get what we expect.

This can be such a mind bender for people that it may take a while to comprehend it. But don't just take my word for it. This is science— quantum physics. I am fascinated with quantum physics but I also appreciate that it is a complex subject, so I will only briefly introduce here the simplified evidence regarding the nature of reality. For those curious souls who love to know all the details, I have more fully explained the chain of events in quantum understanding in the Appendix.

In the 1950s, at the University of London, physicist David Bohm suggested that objective reality does not exist and that despite an apparent solidity the universe is essentially an illusion—a gigantic, intricately detailed and complex holographic illusion. Holograms are fascinating because each part of the image of a hologram contains the entire image; therefore, the whole is in every part.

Scientists had previously decided the universe was made up of particles. Bohm argued that at some deeper level of reality, such particles are not individual entities but are actually extensions of the same fundamental whole, a kind of quantum energy field of pure possibility where everything was somehow connected. As scientists began to study more and more minute levels of matter, they began to see that at the smallest levels, smaller than the atom, there is more space than there is solidity. For example, if you examined this book under a high-powered microscope you would see more space than you would solid matter.

According to quantum field theorists, the atoms of which the book is made are 99.999 percent composed of the void and emptiness of space. The subatomic particles are impulses of energy and information. What gives the appearance of matter is the density of the arrangement and their unique vibratory rate. As you look around you now, everything that you can see and touch is made of the same substance (or nonsubstance)—every person, every object, and every star in the sky.

If the concreteness of the world is but a secondary reality and what you experience is actually a holographic blur of frequencies, and if the brain is also a hologram and only selects some of the frequencies out of this blur to transform them into sensory perceptions, what becomes of objective reality? Put quite simply, it ceases to exist. As the religions of the East have long upheld, the material world is *maya*, an illusion. We are then receivers of information and what we select becomes our physical reality, which is only one possibility taken from an infinite sea of possibilities.

This directly relates to producing wealth and power and anything else you want to have, because the more you understand about the way you interpret information, the more power you have to change your experience. If you don't particularly enjoy your current reality, you have the opportunity to choose an alternative reality from the sea of possibility. In the next two chapters we will take a closer look at all the ways you translate the frequencies of information surrounding you to create your current circumstance. Armed with that awareness, you can choose whatever experience you desire. It is when you begin to focus on those things you want, not on the things you don't want, that you realize how much flexibility and control you innately possess. Then you begin to play life at a whole new level, a level that works for you instead of against you.

Our Individual Experience of the World

Your brain works very much like the World Wide Web. When you go to Yahoo! and search for a specific word or phrase, within a matter of seconds you will be presented with all the possible matches for the criteria you entered. All of the millions of other pages of information are left out. You pulled up only what you were looking for. The search engine translated your request and delivered possible solutions to you based on what you asked for.

Your nervous system works the same way. In the book *Flow*, Hungarian biologist Mihaly Csikszentmihalyi says that you are constantly being bombarded by approximately 2,000,000 bits of information per second via the input channels of your five senses. If you were to be instantaneously aware of this external input all at once, you would undoubtedly go insane. Your nervous system is designed to cut this massive amount of information down into manageable sizes, or "chunks." Out of 2,000,000 bits of information, you actually process only about 134 bits, or seven chunks (plus or minus two, which means five to nine chunks). So you only process .000067 percent of all of the information coming in. We have this incredible ability to impair our own vision, so to speak, just to keep us from getting utterly overwhelmed. As psychologist Ulric Neisser put it, "Our mental machinery knows everything that is going on around us but discards most as unimportant before consciousness is reached."

In the exercise earlier, when you were looking for blue objects, that's what you found. You punched in "blue" to your search engine and your reality came alive with blue objects. If you did the exercise you will have realized that all the other colors around you melted away as you sought out blue because your focus was blue. So when your focus shifted to the other question, you realized you didn't see all of the objects and things that fit that description. Why? Because you were not looking for them. Once again, it's completely dependent on the individual as to what information is processed and what information is not.

Another way to think of it is like this. You live in a dark room. All you've got is one flashlight, which represents your seven (plus or minus two) chunks of awareness mentioned earlier. Remember, you're being bombarded by 2,000,000 bits of information per second and you're only aware of 134 bits per second. Obviously you're deleting an incredible amount of information. All possibilities exist in this dark room. There is poverty, wealth, poor relationships, great relationships, fitness, vitality, illness, disease, happiness, and depression. What becomes your experience of life is what you choose to shine your light of focus on. It is what you pay attention to.

The greatest challenge you have at this moment in terms of accomplishing all of your goals is that approximately 90 percent of the determinants of your focus are still at the unconscious level. All this means is that you may not be aware of what is keeping you from having all that you want. You must first excavate what it is that your unconscious mind is focusing on, so that you can shift that focus to produce better results. What are these unconscious determinants of focus? That's what we are going to look at next.

Question: What things are yellow?

CHAPTER

The Rules of the Game

If a thing is humanly possible,
consider it to be within your reach.

—Marcus Aurelius

Okay, let's just regroup for a second. Suppose that all I have said so far is correct—and I promise you, far greater minds than mine have proven it is. What does it mean for you? It means that you have the opportunity to change any and every aspect of your life, starting *right now!*

What Determines Focus?

I mentioned at the start of the last chapter that two factors govern your experience and that they are were inextricably linked. The first is focus. The second is what I call your rule book, which we will look at now.

As we've seen, your results in life are dictated by what you focus on. But what you focus on is determined by the rules or parameters of your game. And the rules of your game are determined by your internal filters—your own unique, internal system of perceiving the external world that governs your life. I call this your hidden rule book. Your rule book is largely unconscious and is based on learned behaviors and personal experiences that have affected your perspective on life. These experiences caused you to draw conclusions about what can and cannot be done, what should and should not be done, and what is possible or impossible to achieve. The tricky part is that most of us don't even know what our own rules are! How can you be expected to win the game if you don't know the rules?

This is where it gets exciting because you are the one who created this rule book that governs your life. Just as you wrote it, you can rewrite it to support you in moving toward a future that fulfills and inspires you. It may be your Bible, but it may have also become your jailer.

These rules determine what you focus on. Think about it for a moment—if you only process 0.000067 percent of all the information available to you in any second, who or what decides what you process? That's an incredibly finely tuned search engine, so what are you keying in? If you are experiencing poverty, then I hate to have to break this to you, but at some level you are typing in "poverty."

The premise of this book is that nothing is outside of you, and therefore your external world is nothing more than a manifested reflection of your internal world. The paradox is that in order to benefit from that awareness, you must learn to use what is being presented to you in your outside world as a guide to help you understand your own internal thinking—which in turn creates your external world!

F. Scott Fitzgerald once said, "The true mark of intelligence is the ability to hold two apparently opposing ideas in the mind simultaneously." Throughout this book you will be challenged many times as we unravel parts of the paradox. The "Game of Life" diagram and analogy in Chapter 2 provides a framework and a new perspective to understand that your current reality is nothing more than a symptom of your thinking. This book will help you identify the symptoms and give you the knowledge and practical tools to treat the cause—once and for all. From there you can move into whatever future you desire. It's going to be an exciting and often surprising adventure, and if you play at it 100 percent it will change your life.

The first step is to unravel all the complex components that come together to create this all-important rule book. It is this that defines your focus and, therefore, your experience. The good news is, because you created your own rules in the first place, once you know what to look for you can easily access them and recreate them to support you rather than sabotage you.

Are you ready to understand yourself like you never have before? The rest of this chapter is devoted to uncovering all the factors that operate your life as you know it now. How the mind and body work to create your behaviors is awesome and complex, so be prepared to soak in some fascinating information. And just know that once you have gotten through it, you will be that much closer to taking charge of the game you are playing, and then propelling yourself toward ultimate success.

If you *really* believed that by mastering this information, you would change your life forever, how committed would you be? If you *knew* that by following through on the exercises in this book you could have all you desire, how much of yourself would you pour into learning the information? My guess is that you would be *very* committed. Do yourself a favor and be willing to accept the possibility that you truly could have the life you envision for yourself, and commit to this transformation now.

Here we go!

Determinants of Focus: Your Reticular Activating System

Located at the base of the brain, the reticular activating system (RAS) is responsible for a number of functions, but the one we are interested in is called *filtering*. This is the process that determines what you become conscious of, what remains in the forefront of your mind, and what simply disappears into the recesses of your unconscious. The RAS is like your own built-in newspaper editor. It decides what is put on the front page and what is to be put on page 30 or archived before it even hits the press!

Whether you are conscious of it or not, you tell the RAS what to look for. This is one of the reasons it's important to write down goals. This action activates the RAS and tells your brain to look out for opportunities or information that will allow whatever it is you want to become a reality. In addition to the biological filters of the RAS, which are unique to us as a species, you also have internal filters that cause your subjective reality to take form.

The Filtration Process

In order to cut down on the overwhelming amount of information coming in through the five senses, your nervous system does the job of deleting, distorting, and generalizing the information. Deletion, distortions, and generalizations are the techniques your mind uses to reduce the information registering in the conscious mind to a manageable amount based on your ground rules—what you are sorting for, or expect to experience. These are the big-picture techniques that aim to chunk higher, squash together, or remove information from your radar screen.

Deletion

I am sure you have had the experience of planning to buy a new car, a new suit, or a pair of shoes, and the moment you decide on the item, you see it everywhere. If you decided to buy a red Toyota, red Toyotas started appearing in your reality. It wasn't that red Toyotas suddenly manifested everywhere you looked. They were always there; you just didn't see them until they were important to you. You had simply never noticed them before, because up until that point, they weren't significant to you, so you had been deleting them from your experience.

Deleting information is simply the process of leaving out large amounts of data that your rule book has deemed unimportant to your life at this time. An example of a deletion would be the businessman and the fisherman we talked about earlier. The merger of the businessman's company may reach the business press, but if it is of no consequence to the fisherman it will be deleted from his experience or awareness. If, however, the fisherman got tired of getting up so early and decided he would buy and sell stock, and he invested money into the businessman's company, you can guarantee that mention of the merger in the newspaper would then catch his attention because suddenly it *is* important to him. So the RAS added it to his awareness.

Your experience of life is largely dependent upon what you are deleting at any given moment. You get what you focus on and you don't experience the things that you delete.

Distortion

Distortion can often appear as the process of interpreting incoming information as something other than what consensual reality says it is. One form of distortion is seeing, hearing, or feeling something that's not actually there. When you think you hear someone say something that wasn't actually said, that's a distortion.

When Al Gore and George W. Bush were having recounts done of the votes that were cast in Florida to decide the 2000 presidential election, the country was sharply divided on how to proceed. The division was largely based on political affiliation. People who supported the Republican Party *distorted* the situation to support their values and beliefs, while people who supported the Democrats *distorted* everything that occurred to support *their* values and beliefs. Had the situation been reversed and the Democrats won the machine vote, then the distortions would have been reversed as well—the two sides would have simply swapped opinions. This is a classic example of distortion.

As with deletion, the ability to distort is a very important function of the human nervous system. If you weren't able to distort information and you met someone for the first time, you would not recognize the person again later in different clothes or with some other change in appearance. Sometimes your distortions empower you, but sometimes they don't. The game is all about choosing an internal process that is empowering. By taking more control of this otherwise unconscious process, you empower yourself to produce the results that you most desire.

Generalization

The third way you filter information is by generalizing. Generalization is a valuable process because it allows you to remember and categorize things once you've learned them. When you were a child you learned that a certain object is called a chair and is used to sit on. You were then able to generalize that similar objects are also called chairs and are also used to sit on. Without the ability to generalize, you would have to relearn what the object is and the purpose it serves each time you saw a different *type* of chair. Generalizations make up your belief systems, or the specific rules you use to govern your life. If you have a generalization or a belief that "chairs are used to sit on," you will sit on them whenever you need to.

Your generalizations, like the other filtration processes, can serve you well, but they can also limit you. As a simple example, imagine you had a bad experience with a chair when you were younger. What would happen if, say, you sat on a chair that was missing a leg, and you fell down and hurt yourself? As a result, your unconscious mind, in order to protect you in the future, might generalize that all chairs are bad. In a case like that, the process of generalization would actually hinder you, because it might take away choices in the future that involved sitting on chairs.

Many people generalize in ways that eliminate choices for them in life. They form beliefs or rules such as "Money and happiness don't go hand in hand," "I could *never* be successful," "You can't make money without cheating people," or "I could never make a positive global impact." In these cases the generalizing function is used in a disempowering way.

Internal Filters—Your Rule Book for Reality

What you delete, distort, and generalize depends on your internal filters. These filters are your rule book and are created through your upbringing, your environment, and the significant emotional experiences in your life. They determine what you focus on, look for, or sort for, and what is left out of your experience of reality. These filters are composed of values, beliefs, attitudes, memories, decisions, language, and thought patterns called meta programs. As John McCrone writes in *How the Brain Works*, "A person is a collection of memories and habits that shape the moment-to-moment flow of the mind."

As we delve into each internal filter more in depth, it is important that you start to recognize yourself in these categories. Beginning the process of self-awareness is the first step to taking charge of your results. You are creating your own cognitive profile that will help you to see your current mind-set, why you are where you are today. As you read through this section, consider how each filter applies to you specifically.

Which rules do you operate with? There are no overall right or wrong answers, only what is true for you. This not only helps you to understand yourself better but also helps you to recognize certain filters in others, which is useful not only when modeling excellence but in managing and leading people.

Understanding this section will prepare you for Chapter 5, which is all about unearthing your own rule book from the recesses of your unconscious mind, so you can clearly see the rules by which you are currently playing the game of life. Once you have clearly identified where you really are, as depicted in Figure 4.1, and not just where you wish you were, you are in position to make lasting changes. These are the components of personality you will also use in Step 2 to create a cognitive profile of your role models.

Values

The first of the seven internal filters is your values. Values represent what is uniquely important to you, the broader concepts that guide your decisions in life and represent what you stand for, such as family, happiness,

Figure 4.1 What Is Possible for You Now

adventure, stability, creative fulfillment, love, money, recognition, respect, justice, and so on. People's experiences vary based on their range of values. An individual who values wealth will invest time and effort in that area, and his or her experience of life will reflect that. If that same person does not value honesty, then the route to wealth will be very different from that of someone who highly values both wealth and honesty.

What is actually important to you can be more accurately gauged by looking at where you spend your time than by asking yourself what your values are. A good friend came to me for coaching because he wasn't producing the results that he wanted in his physical health. He was a financially successful executive who ran three different companies, but he was running his physical health into the ground. I proceeded to elicit his life values by asking him the question, "What's important to you in life?" He listed a number of different things, including entrepreneurialism and financial success but, interestingly enough, health was not even included on his list. Because his values determined where he spent his time, the root cause of his issue was clearly a values issue. Recognizing this was the first step for him in turning his health around.

Beliefs

The second internal filter is your beliefs. Beliefs are your convictions, those things that you consider true. If you believe that you can learn anything that you put your mind to, regardless of age, your experiences are going to be very different from those people who believe they are not very smart and couldn't possibly learn something new.

Your beliefs form the parameters of your game. They make up some of the boundary conditions of your thinking that Einstein referred to in the quotation that opened Chapter 1. Your beliefs will narrow your possible experiences as fast as any other filter can. When transformed, beliefs can also give wings to your potential and allow you to soar to new heights.

A talented woman who attended one of my seminars told me that she was an artist. She absolutely loved what she did, but she wasn't making the kind of money that she wanted. After doing some exploration, it was revealed that she had a belief that women could not make real money in art. This belief was preventing her from focusing on all the money-making opportunities that existed for her. Identifying the limiting belief was the precursor for obliterating it. Soon after that, her income tripled.

Attitudes

Attitudes, the third set of filters, are abstract ideas made up of clusters of beliefs and values around a given subject. An attitude is a frame of mind built on your values and beliefs. Attitudes are often hard to pin-point because they are less solid and therefore can be quite insidious. They can distort your perspective positively or negatively. When people talk of seeing something through rose-colored glasses, they are referring to a person's attitude. For example, the person who has a positive attitude toward work and sees it as a place to self-actualize while creating value for others will have a very different experience than someone who has a negative attitude toward work and sees it only as a means to pay bills.

A woman came to me once for coaching, stating that she wanted to lose some weight because, she said, it would make her feel better about herself, give her more energy, and positively affect the results she was producing in her career. I suggested that in order to make the changes she wanted to make, she would have to change her eating habits. She was, however, adamant that she wasn't prepared to do that. She apparently assumed that if she worked with a results coach she would be able to miraculously get results without changing anything! I explained the law of cause and effect, where every action creates an equal and opposite reaction. If she didn't change her actions, she couldn't change the results of her actions. She chose not to continue, yet her attitude was the only thing standing between her and the outcome she desired.

Memories

Memories also filter your current experience of reality. You evaluate your world through your memories and the experiences that you have. Memories can be the cement or rationale that keeps a belief in place. Yet they are only stored snapshots of an event that was multidimensional. You only have the leftover remnants of whatever segments of that event you processed through your perceptual filters at that time. For example, let's say that an Alsatian dog ran up to you when you were three years old. You were very scared, because an Alsatian is a large dog. In that moment you made a neurological connection between dogs and being scared. As an adult you may not even remember the incident of being scared by the dog, but you nonetheless feel afraid of dogs. You have used the old memory to ascribe the same or similar meaning to a current situation, which then directs your emotional reaction in the present, even though you may not know why. Someone may ask why you're afraid of dogs, to which you may respond, "I don't know—I just am," as if that fear were just part of your personality you cannot change.

A memory may be 20 years old or more, but it can still trigger your interpretation and perception of the current situation based on your subjective generalized memory of the original incident. One gentleman in our seminars mentioned that when he was growing up, his parents were constantly arguing about money. Because he had no other references to prove otherwise, he mentally linked the two ideas together and formed the conclusion that money equaled unhappiness. As a result, he made an unconscious choice never to have any money, since that was what spoiled relationships. With the techniques presented in this book, he was able to expand his positive references and thus expand his playing field and change the game he was playing to include relationships and an abundance of money.

Decisions

Decisions are also one of the major filters of your experience. Throughout your life you make decisions, both consciously and unconsciously, as to the meaning of the things that happen in your subjective reality. If memories are the cement that perpetuates a belief, then decisions are the cornerstones of belief. They act as the line in the sand from which you will make future choices. Every belief is preceded by either a conscious or unconscious decision to accept that belief.

Someone who decides early in life that he or she will one day become President of the United States of America will have a different experience of life than someone who decides that he or she will never amount to anything. A woman in one of my seminars had made a decision at an early age that "this is a man's world" and she would have to struggle and work many times harder in order to achieve only moderate success. Therefore, she continually sorted for, or looked for, every example in her experience that would back up the decision she had already made unconsciously about life. We tend to get what we look for. Her present life reflected a decision she had made a long time ago. This all changed for her in one of our weekend seminars when she used the Neurological Repatterning™ tools to obliterate the limiting decision.

Language

Language is also a powerful filter. Linguist Max Muller states it this way: "We can as little think without words as we can breathe without lungs." The language that you use can actually determine what concepts are available to you, and therefore your experience in life. Analytical philosophers and linguists as varied as Arthur Schopenhauer and Max Muller have all stressed the point that language is what allows us to take our mind and consciousness to previously unexplored places.

An animal such as a cat or a dog can only think in relation to the present tense. For example, a cat cannot imagine what it might be doing two days from now. Language allows human beings to transport themselves mentally to imagined viewpoints or even to consider how we might be perceived from other points of view. Because language determines what we can think about, it also determines what we see in the world.

Ludwig Wittgenstein once said, "Whereof one cannot speak, one cannot think." I saw an amazing demonstration of this once on a television talk show on which a Native American Indian chief was being interviewed. He mentioned that his tribe had no word in its language for "war"—therefore, he emphasized, the concept of war did not exist for them.

If you want to be rich, one of the things you need to do is to increase your financial vocabulary. The moment you begin to increase your financial vocabulary, you begin to open up the limits you have placed on your experience, and thus shift your focus and expand your playing field. How can you think like an investor if you don't know the language of investing? Business and investing have a language of their own.

Understanding financial ratios and financial statements requires an awareness of the terms associated with them. When you understand the terms, your mind can think in new ways that were previously unavailable.

I had a friend who was taught early in life that one shouldn't speak about financial matters because it was inappropriate and money was not important. His parents told him relationships and love were more important than money. I don't necessarily disagree with that idea, but who says you can't have both? Because he never discussed money, he never learned how to think in financial terms and, consequently, found himself without money.

How do you increase your financial vocabulary? Read new types of materials; have new conversations with people. Warren Buffett, the world's most successful investor, was once asked to reveal the secret of his success, and he replied, "I read over two thousand annual reports a year."

Meta Programs

Meta programs are the last set of filters that determine your experience of the world. They are context-dependent, content-free thought and behavioral patterns, or programs, that determine your experience in life. I list several meta programs in the pages that follow, along with descriptions of each of the patterns. As you read these descriptions, consider how you filter the world using each meta program. To gain a better understanding of how you operate, circle the option within each meta program category that best describes how you function. Beginning to recognize how these filters affect what you do and how you do it will give you a more comprehensive picture of why you are or aren't getting certain results.

This will also provide you invaluable insight into how and why others operate the way they do. This knowledge, which very few people have, will help you know how to communicate more effectively, hire, lead, and motivate others. This aspect of the cognitive profile is also very important when applying Cognitive Reimprinting™, as you'll see in Chapter 7.

Motivation Filter
Do you move primarily *toward* what you want in life or *away from* what you don't want? If you are propelled toward what you want, then positive statements like "Money will give me freedom and a sense of

achievement" will motivate you. If you move away from what you don't want, negatively expressed statements such as "Money will mean I'll never be broke again" will motivate you.

Away-from motivation can provide a powerful push, but it will tend to produce inconsistent results, for a couple of different reasons. If your primary motivation is "not wanting to be broke" or "having to pay the bills," you are actually focused on "being broke" and "paying the bills." The unconscious mind cannot process a negative statement directly. So in this instance, if I say, "I don't want to be broke," the brain must first think about being broke in order to think about *not* being broke. Because we tend to get what we focus on in life, if "being broke" or "paying the bills" is your focus, this will tend to be all that you experience.

Also, from a motivation perspective, seeking money because you "don't want to be broke" or because you "have to pay the bills" is called pain-motivated performance. Pain-motivated performance will still push you, but the moment you are no longer broke (if you are lucky enough to make it there) or the moment that you have paid all the bills, your motivation disappears. This will tend to cause cyclical performance. On the other hand, if you are extremely toward motivation, you may never get around to doing the things that are necessary for the maintenance of the result.

In order to determine whether you are toward or away-from motivated, think about a short- or long-term goal, then ask yourself the question, "What is important to me about achieving that goal?" Notice whether your responses are primarily rooted in what you want or what you don't want. Then decide which of these describes your pattern of motivation:

- Toward motivated
- Toward with a little away
- Both toward and away equally
- Away with a little toward
- Away from motivated

Orientation Filter
This filter is similar to the motivation filter, although it is more about whether you do what you do because of the possibilities you look

forward to or out of a sense of necessity or obligation. If you are necessity oriented, you will tend to operate based upon what you are "supposed to" do or "should" do, whereas if you are possibility oriented you will tend to act based upon what you "can" do or "could" accomplish.

The question you can ask yourself in order to determine whether you are primarily possibility or necessity oriented is, "Why am I choosing to do what I'm doing in my career?" Notice if your response tends more toward a sense of possibility or necessity, or both in equal measure. Which of the following describes your orientation?

- Possibility
- Necessity
- Both

Success Indicator Filter

This filter determines how you evaluate your performance. Do you look for external verification on how you are doing, or do you just know inside yourself how you've done? Are you more concerned with what others think or with what you think? The question to determine your frame of reference is, "What or who lets me know I've done a good job?" Notice whether your answer is based on internal or external indicators, and choose which of the following best fits:

- Internal
- External
- Internal with external check
- External with internal check

Decision-Making Filter

This filter determines what internal representation system you use to make a decision. Do you have to *see* evidence that convinces you, *hear* the evidence, *read* about it, or prove it to yourself by *doing* it? This filter will also tend to determine how you know you've truly learned something. Ask yourself, "What do I need in order to make my decision about a proposal? Do I have to see it, hear about it, read about it, or do it with them?" Circle the one that is most essential to you:

- See
- Hear
- Read
- Do

Convincer Filter

This filter determines how often you need to go through your decision-making strategy before you are convinced of anything. We all have unconscious strategies for making decisions, which are simply the order and sequence of steps that need to occur in order for us to make a given decision. The convincer filter is determined by asking yourself, "How many options do I need to weigh before I can make a choice?" Are you able to make a decision immediately? Do you decide after looking at a couple of options? Do you need a certain period of time before you can make a decision about something, or do you need to be consistently convinced? Which of the following best describes your decision-making process?

- Able to decide automatically
- Need to consider it a number of times
- Need a period of time
- Need to be consistently convinced

Leadership Filter

This filter demonstrates whether you know what you need to do in order to be successful at any given task, if you know what others need to do, and if you find it easy or not so easy to tell others what they should do. If you categorize your leadership ability as "self only," it means you are effective at leading your own life, although you may not be able to manage others because you don't find it easy to tell them what to do. If you choose "self and others," you are able to lead your own life as well as manage and direct others. "Self but not others" means you know what you need to do in order to be successful, but you have no idea what other people need to do; therefore you will certainly have difficulty leading other people. Finally, a leadership filter of "others only" indicates you have no idea what you need to do to be successful, but you know what everyone else needs to do. Ask yourself the question, "What could I do to improve my performance at work?" and then, "What could my coworkers do?" If you find it easier to know what others could improve on than how you could improve, then ask yourself, "Could I easily *tell* them what they could improve on?" Then choose which of the following filters best fits your answers:

- Self only
- Self and others
- Self but not others
- Others only

Energy Direction Filter

This filter will determine where you direct your energy when pursuing your life goals. You are generally either more active or more reflective in life. If you are at the far extreme of activity you will take massive action toward your goals, so much so that sometimes you will jump into the pool and then check to see if there is water in it afterwards. If you are more reflective you will tend to do a detailed study of all the consequences of action before taking it. Reflection at its extreme can lead to the paralysis of analysis, where no action is taken and you just sit back and let the world pass you by. Ask yourself the question, "When I come into a new situation, do I usually take action immediately or do I conduct a detailed study of all of the consequences before acting?"

Are you:

- Active
- Reflective
- Both
- Inactive

Performance Filter

This is different from the energy direction filter in that it speaks more of where you gain your greatest pleasure in your career path, and therefore where you perform optimally. Do you prefer situations in which you are a solo or independent player? Do you prefer to be part of a team or do you prefer to lead a team? Ask yourself the question, "What gives me the greatest enjoyment at work—when I am working on my own, as part of a team, or when I am leading a team?"

What kind of player are you?

- Independent player
- Team player
- Management player

Work Satisfaction Filter

Do you prefer to work with things, systems, or people? If you like to work with *people*, you will often describe the joys of interacting with others when talking about work. If you are more inclined to work with *systems*, you will often talk about the systems in place that make work compelling. If you get satisfaction from working with *things*, you might talk about the specific things you do when describing your work. Ask yourself the question, "What do I particularly enjoy about what I do for work?"

- Things
- Systems
- People

Preferred Interest Filter

The preferred interest filter is similar to the work satisfaction filter, although it relates more to what you focus on in life, rather than from a work perspective specifically. Ask yourself, "What do I enjoy spending my time doing?" Do you think more about the people you spend time with, the places you go or live, the things or objects you come in contact with, the activities you take part in, or the information and learning you gather? Which of these describes your primary interests?

- People
- Places
- Things

- Activities
- Information

Abstract/Specific Filter

Are you an abstract thinker or do you operate more on the plane of specificity? If abstract, you see the big picture. At the extreme of this range we might find the spiritual person who is interested only in the relationship with God, love, or light. At the other end of the spectrum would be the accountant who is only interested in numbers.

The way you chunk information holds a direct relationship to the amount of money that you make in life. In a business setting, the global thinker has the big picture and will often be the CEO, entrepreneur, planner, politician, or visionary. The specific thinker will tend to be the assistant taking care of the details or the janitor. The trick, however, is to be able to move throughout the range from abstract thinking to specific thinking. Some abstract thinkers are not sufficiently grounded to produce results in the material world. The magician of the material world is the person who can weave the abstract vision, then take action and apply it with enough specificity to produce real-world results.

Ask yourself the question, "What are my future goals?" Then see if you focus on the big picture and abstract feelings, or on specific numbers of how much you want to be worth and certain things you want to have along the way. Finally, see if your mind moves from the big picture to the specifics or vice versa. Choose the term that describes your focus:

- Specific
- Abstract
- Specific to abstract
- Abstract to specific

Comparison Filter

This filter relates to what relationships you tend to see between people and how you compare things. Do you look for the similarities or the differences? The sameness person will tend to like routines. This individual does not care for change but finds security and comfort in sameness. The differences person, on the other hand, is someone who craves variety and will tend to notice the differences in things.

Look at Figure 4.2 and ask yourself the question, "What's the relationship between these three coins?" Notice whether you focus on the similarities or differences. Choose the term that best describes your focus:

- Sameness
- Sameness with exceptions
- Sameness with differences equally
- Differences with similarities
- Differences

Challenge Response Filter

Are you a feeling person who tends to let your feelings run your life, or are you more dissociated and thinking in your approach? Another possibility is that you could have a choice and operate in either thinking or feeling mode at will. Recall an event in your career that gave you trouble or was personally challenging to you, and ask yourself, "Did I react in a way that was more feeling, thinking, or did I have a choice between the two?" Choose the word that best describes your style:

- Thinking
- Feeling
- Choice

Time Awareness Filter

Do you plan your life out or live freely in the moment, taking each day as it comes? If you are a *through time* person, you tend to be very time

Figure 4.2 Test for Comparison Filter

conscious. You live life in relation to time, don't tend to be late, and have a good idea of your goals or ambitions or the direction you're heading in life. You likely have your goals mapped out on a time line. If you are an *in time* person, on the other hand, you are more interested in living in the moment. You have less direction and care more about fully experiencing the now, which can mean you are often late and have less awareness of time. Choose which term best describes your approach:

- Through time
- In time

Focus Filter

This final meta program relates to whether you are primarily focused on yourself or other people. A major airline used this filter when they were hiring staff. During the interview process, the candidates were asked to stand in front of the group, one by one, and give a short presentation on themselves. What the candidates were not aware of was that they were being monitored, based not on how well they spoke or presented, but on how well they listened to the other candidates when they spoke. It was a brilliant strategy for hiring naturally service-oriented people. All of the candidates were under pressure to perform and do their best, so this exercise tested whether they were more interested in themselves and how well they would do, or whether they still focused on those around them.

Where does your focus lie?

- Self
- Others

Your values, as well as your beliefs, attitudes, and meta programs, are instilled at an early age, based upon those of your parents and whether you accepted or rejected theirs. Many of these filters change as you grow older, and they continue to be shaped by society, peer influences, and significant emotional events. Figure 4.3 summarizes the filters and their influence on perception. This rule book of beliefs, values, and other filter patterns that you have created is real, but only to

Internal Filters

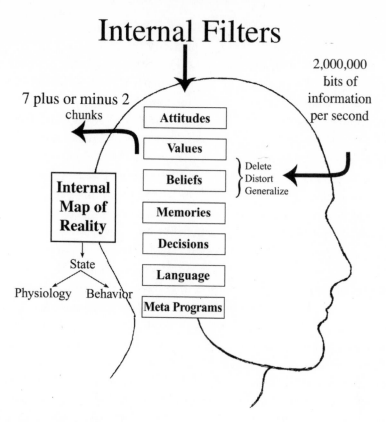

Figure 4.3 Model of Filtration

you as an individual. Your model of the world is as unique as your thumbprint.

All of your internal filters affect your life dramatically. Let's look at beliefs for a moment. It does not matter whether a belief is true, right, or real. What is important is whether or not a belief that you hold produces the results you want in your life. A belief is nothing more than a generalization about the world or your ability, which then determines what behaviors and actions you allow yourself to experience. For every idea there is always a counterexample that could prove it untrue. It's important to understand that generalizations and beliefs are all just opinions—including this one. So the question to ask is, are my beliefs creating the behaviors and experiences that I prefer? Most people think that the world they experience is unchangeable. I hope that, having read the previous chapter, you are starting to see that this need not be the case.

Think about it. If somebody says that the reason they are not successful is because they didn't go to college, the presupposed belief is that people who don't go to college are unsuccessful and that people who do go to college are successful. This generalization does not hold true, yet it has the potential of giving a person a reason or excuse not to explore certain options in life and excel. A person has that belief may not go after a high-paying job because he or she believes those are reserved for people who have gone to college. This type of thinking can limit the results that you produce in life by preventing certain avenues from being explored. If Bill Gates had the belief that one needs a degree to be successful, he might not have dropped out of Harvard to start Microsoft and become the richest man in the world 11 years later. There are many examples of people who have gone to college and become very successful. There are also countless examples of those who never got a degree but went on to be multimillionaires. And then there are people who have graduated from college and been spectacular failures. The point is, whether you did or didn't get an education is not what will stop you from achieving your dreams. What matter are the results that you produce by either having the belief or not having it. What can and will stop you from succeeding are the limiting beliefs that make it okay for you to not even try.

Simply educating yourself and learning new things can have the effect of changing your internal filters. For example, the more I learned about personal finances, the more it became important to me to create wealth in my life. This changed my values considerably. The more I learned about how to produce results in the world, the more I realized the true power that we can all access. At that point, I felt a responsibility to help shape the world in positive ways and make sure that as many people as possible get this information and these skills of empowerment. It is possible to change your mind's through and behavior patterns through education.

It is important to remember that although the processes of deletion, distortion, and generalization are your first-cut techniques for defining reality, they are inextricably linked to the more detailed filters, because it is the unique combination of these finer filters that determines what you will delete, distort, and generalize. This has tremendous significance, because when you realize that what you consider to be real in your experience is only a fraction of what's really out there, you begin to redirect your focus and actually choose what appears in your reality. You then begin to gain control over what you sort for or look for and, therefore, what you experience in life. Your experience becomes more positive and in line with what you desire.

What Rules Are You Playing By?

We do not see things as they are;
we see things as we are.

—The Talmud

Before we explore what your particular rules are, I want to explain a couple of exciting things. The first is the concept that *perception is projection*.

Perception Is Projection

Psychologists since Freudian times have spoken of the concept of *projection* and have stated that "perception is projection." Essentially, what this means is that you can't see anything outside of you that isn't you. So examining an area of your life that you are currently not happy with can yield extraordinary insights about what you believe about life. If, for example, you don't have as much money as you would like, this is a clear indication that at some level you have one or more limiting beliefs about money. You may not be consciously aware of them, but they are there. Once you know they are there, you can set about uncovering them and bringing them into awareness. Simply by doing that, you cause the limiting beliefs to lose their power over you. You can then start to create new results in the realm of wealth creation.

Change Your Mind, Change Your World

I encourage you to see your current life as a reflection of your thinking, a benchmark of your own psychological understanding and strength. Your experience is an accurate and ruthless measure of what you are currently communicating to the universe about who you are and what you will and will not accept in your life. This is your opportunity to use your circumstances and situations as a way of understanding yourself better. And that is empowering. If you can use your so-called failings as a compass pointing toward success, you will reach your destination in a fraction of the time. You no longer just hope that you are going in the right direction while running blindly down alley after alley; instead, you plot a true course.

The reason this is so important and so powerful is that once you start to unpack your life, you can look more clearly at different areas and see what is working and what is not. Both hold clues to your ultimate success.

Over the past decade I have taught seminars around the world and worked with many thousands of people. One thing that constantly fascinates me is that people are basically the same, no matter their culture, color, or creed. One of the most disempowering similarities I have found time and time again is the blanket generalizations that people place over their own lives. Naturally, those who are looking for change are usually the people that wind up in one of my programs. And those same individuals who are not achieving at the level they know they're capable of are simply being held back by their own stuck mind-set. I absolutely applaud every one of them, because they have taken a critical first step toward changing their mind, and therefore their experience, as have you in reading this book.

So let's first get a clear picture of where you are in the pursuit of your dreams now. I have noticed that as I talk with people about what their lives are currently like, often the response is something like, "Oh it's terrible, nothing is working." Yet, when I press for specifics, they are able to see that it's not actually true that *nothing* is working, just certain areas of their life. And there may very well be areas that they are completely overlooking as positive. For example, they may be happily married, have a wonderful relationship with their children, or be very fit and healthy, yet these areas are ignored as they strive for more money in the bank or the next promotion. Right now I want you to get clear about what areas of your life are working and which ones don't appear to be working at the level you would like. Know that both are very powerful, as they each provide signposts for improvement, which I will explain along the way.

Based on my experience, I have categorized the various areas of life that most people are interested in. With each one I want you to be honest and give yourself a score from 1 to 10, 10 being the highest sense of satisfaction and success, 1 being the lowest. If other areas spring to mind for you, add them.

_____   Relationship/love
_____   Family life
_____   Financial
_____   Health and fitness
_____   Contribution in the community
_____   Spiritual growth
_____   Friendships
_____   Career
_____   _____
_____   _____

This exercise should give you some perspective about what you want to change, what currently works or doesn't work, what you want to improve and focus on, and what you are content with as it is. This information will help you as you continue through the book. Knowing your starting point is the first step to mapping out where you want to go and the best way to get there.

You can now do the following exercise on any of the categories above or, as will be explained, on your life as a whole. I encourage you to run the exercise on separate categories and compare the highest-scoring category with the lowest-scoring category. This can be incredibly useful as it lets you see the beliefs that form the basis for your experience. You will no doubt discover that the areas of your life that work better are those areas supported by empowering, healthy values and beliefs. Those areas that don't work are not.

Determine Your Hidden Rule Book

Part of getting what you want and getting where you want to go is knowing where you are now. You have already identified your meta programs, which are part of your rule book. Now it's time to take a closer look at the rest of the components that make up your subjective experience of reality. As you do the following exercise, be honest with yourself.

We'll start with your life values. Ask yourself the question, "What's important to me in life?" Values are distinctly different from goals in that they are usually the qualities behind what you are seeking, or why you do what you do. For example, a politician could seek office for different reasons—in pursuit of justice or in pursuit of fame or varying degrees of both depending on what's important to her. Make a complete list of your top values below. Your responses should be single words or short phrases:

_____

_____

_____

_____

_____

_____

_____

Once you've listed all of your values, or what's important to you, it's time to number them from one to 10 in order of decreasing importance. When you do this, make sure you order them the way they really are, not the way you wish they were. This is the key distinction. For example, if you say that wealth is your number one value but you spend your time playing Nintendo all day, most likely wealth isn't really your number one value. Maybe freedom, fun, or relaxation is more important to you than you thought. Because values provide our up-front motivation, it's likely that you are either actualizing your highest values or spending a good portion of your time on them. Remember, values differ from goals in that goals require steps to achieve them while your values are something you live every day. So place the values you stated earlier in order of importance below, according to which are actually showing up in your life the most and least.

1. _____

2. _____

3. _____

4. _____

5. _____

6. _____

7. _____

8. _____

9. _____

10. _____

When people list their values in their true order of importance, as you have just done, it can be an eye-opener and even disillusioning. Disillusionment is good. It's the first step toward making the changes you desire.

Next, I want you to write down three outrageous goals—three results that you would desire if you had no limits and you could live your wildest dreams. Write down one in the context of your life's path, one in the context of your finances, and one in the context of what you would like to contribute to the world.

1. Life's path

_____

_____

_____

_____

_____

_____

2. Finances

_____

_____

_____

_____

_____

3. Contribution to the world

_____

_____

_____

_____

_____

_____

Once you've written down the three goals, the next step is to write down everything that is preventing you from achieving those goals. For example, you might say, "I'm too young," "I'm too old," "I don't have the education," or "I don't have the resources or contacts I need." These are the boundary conditions of your thinking, or your limiting beliefs.

Because your beliefs have such a huge effect on what you will ultimately experience in your life, it is important to see clearly what they are.

When you think about your beliefs, you will find that many of your assumptions about life have been handed down to you by your family. Others may have come from your own experience. This is an illuminating process for most people. Often we are genuinely shocked by some of the things that spring to mind regarding our ability and worthiness to be, do, and have all we desire. These beliefs have been cobbled together and taken as true, often without your conscious awareness. But because you are the one who accepted these rules, you are on your way to choosing now to change your mind and install a new rule book. For now, make a list of everything that is currently preventing you from achieving those three goals.

_____

_____

_____

_____

_____

Next, it's time to discover some of your traits and attitudes. List below the traits that you believe those who know you well would describe you as having.

_____

_____

_____

_____

Now list the attitudes that you would describe yourself as having, specifically in relationship to your life's path, your career, and your finances. Remember to be honest with yourself. This is not the place to highlight only your positive attitudes. They are relevant, too, so include them. However, use this as an opportunity to unearth your negative attitudes and expectations as well. These are some of the inner obstacles you will want to move beyond.

_____

_____

_____

_____

Congratulations! You are making real progress toward the wealth and power you desire. It's been said that a problem well-stated is a problem half-solved. Understanding your own hidden rule book, which has up to this point been unconscious, empowers you to change your rules, change the terrain, and change the results of your game. Your next step is to decide what game you want to play instead and master the new rules!

STEP

Choose Your Game

Model the Change You Want to Be

Most everything I've done,
I've copied from someone else!
—Sam Walton, founder of Wal-Mart

As natural as Oprah Winfrey seems at what she does, there was a time when she was completely insecure and had to go through a period of trial and error before she had a basis from which to launch her own unique style and niche. She has said, "When I did my first audition for my first television job, I was such a nervous wreck, I had no idea what to do or say. And I thought in my head that maybe I'll just pretend I'm Barbara Walters. I will sit like Barbara and hold my head like Barbara. So, I crossed my legs at the ankles, I put my little finger under my chin, I leaned across the desk, and I pretended to be Barbara Walters."

Modeling is something you have been doing your whole life without being aware of it. The only problem is that most of us model haphazardly, without conscious awareness. Over the course of these next three chapters you will learn how to consciously choose who you want to model and rapidly take on those behaviors and strategies to propel you toward the success you desire.

As I mentioned in the Introduction, Sir Isaac Newton once said,

"The reason I see so far is because I stand on the tall shoulders of those who came before me." Modeling is a specific tool that, when fully applied, can launch you toward tremendous success. Take the classic book *Think and Grow Rich*, for example. Napoleon Hill, on encouragement from Andrew Carnegie, dedicated his life to studying the great players of the time. He modeled their behavior and attempted to describe their methods and their minds so that the information could be synthesized and used by every man and woman willing to play a bigger game full out. The great news is that with today's advanced technologies and understanding of the brain, you can accelerate that process tenfold. Think of *Turning Passions into Profits* as a modern version of *Think and Grow Rich!*

We have established the fact that your experience of reality is based on your internal blueprint of reality. You project your reality by seeing or experiencing only that which you are conditioned or taught to look for. But you actually live in a quantum soup of pure potentiality, which means you only experience the world that you are conditioned to see until you expand your mind and learn to look through new eyes. Once you do this, then you realize there are other potential realities, other aspects of the game you could be playing. You are not destined to remain on the same playing field unless you choose to. The choice is yours. You can design your own destiny.

The best way to learn a new aspect of the game or to improve your ability to play your current game is to seek out those who have already mastered it, find out how they did it, and follow in their footsteps. This is the natural process known as role modeling.

Role modeling is something that you have done unconsciously from the time you were born. According to sociologist Dr. Morris Massey, role modeling is responsible for many of your values and beliefs about life. And it is these role-modeled opinions and ideas that form the basis of your rule book.

According to Dr. Massey, you go through three major developmental stages:

1. 0 to 7 years old: the imprint period
2. 7 to 14 years old: the modeling period
3. 14 to 21 years old: the socialization period

Ages zero to seven are considered the imprint period. During this time you became almost a cookie-cutter imprint of your parents. You unconsciously modeled the values of your parents and you emulated them in most every way. Outside influences such as the culture that your family lived in also played a role in the development of your values at this early age. Certain cultural values are indigenous to the people that live within the culture.

Were you raised with a religious background, and if so, what religion? Did your parents care for you exclusively or did you have a nanny? If you had a nanny, what were your nanny's values and attitudes? All of these things contributed to the development of your values at this early age.

In this developmental period, as well as the two that follow, Dr. Massey also points to what he calls significant emotional events, which play a major role in the development of values. Was there abuse or trauma in your past? What significant events were occurring in the environment around you? A child who grew up during the Great Depression may have acquired significantly different values than someone who grew up during a time of great prosperity within the country.

Ages 7 to 14 are said by Dr. Massey to be the modeling period. During this time you began to find role models either inside or outside of the family. Family role models might include older brothers or sisters. Other children at school and their values also influenced you. You found heroes and were greatly influenced by the values of those heroes. Interestingly enough, the media could have had a major impact at this young age, through the types of heroes portrayed in movies or the personalities of the rock stars that you emulated.

What were your heroes' attitudes? When the James Bond movies first came out, how did the character of Bond affect and shape the values of the young men who looked upon him as a hero? How do some of the rock stars of this generation affect and influence the values of our children today? Dr. Massey believes that to a large extent, who you are today and the types of goals you set in life are often a result of the types of heroes you had when you were 10 years old.

The last of the developmental periods, as Dr. Massey describes them, is the socialization period. Your socialization period occurred between the ages of 14 and 21, when you were in the process of fully integrating values, beliefs, and filter systems into your personality. All the outside influences, including media, family, friends, geography, culture, religion, significant emotional events, and so forth, continued to have an affect on the values system that you eventually made your own. Dr. Massey believes that in the early 20s, young adults tend to go through a period of experimentation, often in the college years. They test out behaviors and ways of viewing the world that sometimes seem to oppose their values. Once they have done that, they tend to revert back to acting in ways that are consistent with the values they hold intrinsically. Dr. Massey states that after this stage, a person's values tend to remain the same, potentially only altered in the presence of a significant emotional event.

The next stage, ages 21 to 35, is the development of the business persona and was defined by William James. The first people you work for may have a big impact on you in terms of your business values and behavior. It is these initial employers that will have the biggest impact on your work ethic.

These stages depict a long, gradual process of developing your values and internal blueprint of reality, which in turn determines the game you are playing and the rules you play by. However, over the last decade, my focus has been largely on the study of accelerated human change, and several techniques that I teach in my programs can assist you to change your values at will for the purpose of creating the life you want. This can also be done to a certain extent through studying someone you consciously choose to model. Role modeling is a natural way for us to learn, yet when we become adults we often stop using it. How to do it effectively with volition is the subject of these next few chapters. Choosing your role models then applying the collection of techniques and principles outlined throughout the rest of the book form the basis of Cognitive Reimprinting™, the *software* that upgrades your mental, physical, and emotional functioning toward optional performance.

Inside and Outside Modeling

Microsoft's dominant position arose from an operating system closely modeled on a Digital Research product and the graphical user interface technology invented at Xerox.
—**Martin S. Fridson**

There are two types of modeling: inside and outside modeling. Outside modeling is surface-level modeling and is much like imitation. When Elvis Presley modeled the best blues singers of his time, he simply watched what they did and mimicked it. He did the same thing when he modeled Roy Orbison's vocal qualities. This is the same type of modeling that Greg Luganis did when he was modeling Johnny Weissmuller's dives, and the same type of modeling that Rupert Murdoch did with British tabloid journalism. Outside modeling can be quite effective, but it is only the tip of the iceberg in terms of what is possible. To really grasp the power of modeling it's best to do both kinds.

Inside modeling is the process of doing complete cognitive profiles on the people you wish to emulate, so as to integrate aspects of their personalities into your own. When you do outside modeling you can pick up surface-level strategies. When you do inside modeling as taught here, you can actually get the masters' entire hidden rule books and the potential of accelerating your success a thousandfold. Inside modeling is the process of taking on their rules for the game of life, as well as expanding your playing field by expanding your references.

So if you are currently playing a game you don't want to play anymore, or playing one badly, wouldn't it make sense to alter the blueprint? Who says that the role modeling you did as a child was all you could do? Who says that you have to accept your lot and be content with survival or mediocrity? Who says that scarcity and failure have to be part of the program? If these things are in your reality, then someone somewhere told you, either verbally or through their actions, that this was the nature of the game. You accepted it—but you didn't have to.

In its simplest form, modeling allows you access to the tools, strategies, and mind-sets of successful people so that you can expand your references and play a different game of life on a larger and more exciting Playing Field. "Fake it until you make it" is a long-held paradigm for success. Far from being dishonest, this principle simply harnesses the power of the mind for accelerated change. Your mind does not know the difference between something that has happened and something you vividly imagined. By identifying the new beliefs, values, attitudes, and decisions that have already worked for someone else you get the inside knowledge of the rules by which to play your new game. Then you can set out to master the same skills and employ the same strategies. Why reinvent the wheel when you can learn from the best of the best? These individuals have become masters because they have crafted their rule book and congruently communicated their vision to the world. They have been clear about who they are, what they stand for, and what they want to achieve, and they have confidently expected to achieve it. You can do the same.

Key Components of a Cognitive Profile

I am 15 percent Phillip Fisher and
85 percent Benjamin Graham.
                                    —Warren Buffett

Now that you understand the importance of modeling as a technique to fast-track your success, let's look at exactly how to do it faster than ever before possible. The first step is to find someone who is playing a game worth playing. Find a role model of excellence. If you choose to model mediocrity, you will end up reproducing mediocrity.

When searching for a role model, ask yourself, "Who is producing the results in life that I want to produce?" Find the person or people who are playing the game you want to play. Learn their rules and incorporate them into your own life. If Gandhi had played by the same rules as the rest of the world, he never would have produced the results that he did. If Richard Branson played by the same rules as the rest of the world, he never would have become the billionaire he is today.

You need to look at what these models are producing, and then play by their rules. You need to find out what's going on inside them cognitively that allows them to produce their result. What are the beliefs, values, decisions, attitudes, and other filter patterns that make up their personality?

The best way to model a result is to find a person who is successfully producing the result you want, and question and observe the person directly. A common excuse for not doing this is, "But why would that person speak to me? How could I possibly impose on this person?" Understand you don't have to go to Branson first off. Find someone in your local community who is playing a game you want to play. Perhaps you know a couple who have a wonderful marriage. Maybe there is a guy two doors down who religiously works out and has a body you admire. Perhaps there is a marketing award winner at work whom you could approach if your ability as a marketer is something you want to improve. Or a relative running their own home-based business who will give you their business plan. Being humble enough to ask will get you further faster than acting as if you already know everything.

There is always more to learn. Get creative and ask. I guarantee everyone loves to be admired, and all the successful people I have ever approached have been thrilled and excited that I was interested enough to ask. Everyone loves to share his or her story.

The second-best way to model excellence is to compile information from various sources about your subject. Go into your local bookshop and have a look at the biography section. If you can't reach Branson personally, read his biography. Research the people you are interested in through interviews, articles, and television documentaries. You should aim to read at least four to six books on each person you want to model, and watch at least four television interviews or programs featuring that person so you can model his or her external behavior and mannerisms. I will show you how to do much of the modeling process very quickly using a master strategy for genius reading. This will allow you to speed through the books with ease.

An accurate model can often be produced from a combination of sources when you don't have access to the actual person. The important thing about the modeling process is to create a useful road map for replicating excellence in any particular game. Whether the model is real or right is irrelevant. The fact remains that when you follow the model or the rule book of this successful person, you can learn exactly how to produce the same results.

What to Watch For

In Chapter 6 we talked about the difference between inside and outside modeling. The quote I used there from Oprah Winfrey is an example of outside modeling:

> *When I did my first audition for my first television job, I was such a nervous wreck, I had no idea what to do or say. And I thought in my head that maybe I'll just pretend I'm Barbara Walters. I will sit like Barbara and hold my head like Barbara. So, I crossed my legs at the ankles, I put my little finger under my chin, I leaned across the desk, and I pretended to be Barbara Walters.*

You can isolate the nuances of external behaviors by watching the person you wish to emulate on television. The Biography Channel is a great source for this sort of information. Notice the similarities of behavior that are consistent. Like Oprah in her earlier days, notice the little things that make that person excellent, and mimic that. When I first read that excerpt, I thought, "If it's good enough for Oprah, it's good enough for me!"

Then there is the inside modeling, which is figuring out how that person thinks. Again, a great deal of this information can be deduced from interviews and books. For inside modeling, the things to watch for are all the internal filters I described in Chapter 4. At that point, the purpose was for you to wake up to how these filters operate in you. Here I will examine each of them again for the purpose of demonstrating how they operate in highly successful people to produce amazing results. This section will show you exactly what kinds of things to be looking for when modeling your particular version of success.

I'm covering in more depth here some of the information from Chapter 4 for two reasons: (1) the mind learns through repetition, and (2) your internal filters are such an integral part of your personality that they are deleting, distorting and generalizing this information even now as you read this! Most people tend to think that everyone else is operating by the same rules. It's extremely important you understand that your unique internal filters are *not* fixed aspects of your personality. You have power over them, not the other way around.

This section will provide you with fresh reference points outside your experience—what combination of internal filters work effectively in successful people, which you have the option to install in yourself for more optimal results.

And remember, you don't necessarily have to like every aspect of the people you model. You can pick and choose which areas of their lives you want to replicate and which you don't. Maybe they are great at negotiating, but you disagree with their values. That's okay. Keep some things and not others. It's all up to you. Here we will reveal the internal filters operating in some of the most outrageously successful and powerful individuals in the world.

Values

A major key to replicating excellence is to uncover what values drive your role models. What's most important to them to get out of life? Branson, for example, values living life to its fullest and having fun. He also values entrepreneurialism and challenge. Oprah values making a difference. Donald Trump values being tough and winning. Celine Dion values being the best, while Madonna values recognition.

Values sculpt the game you play, to the extent that the actions you take and decisions you make are motivated by the desire to attain your highest values. When you are modeling people, watch for them to reveal their values through their personal descriptions of life, their passions, and how they spend their time. What end-result quality inspites their actions?

Beliefs

Rupert Murdoch, primary shareholder of News Corporation and one of the most powerful men on the planet, was quoted during his rise to the top as having said, "There is no question that we will be successful. The only question is what level of success we will attain." This belief supported his success and propelled him forward.

Oprah has repeated on numerous occasions her belief that "excellence is the best deterrent to racism and sexism." This belief has allowed her to excel where others settled for mediocrity.

Warren Buffett holds a belief that it's easier to create money than to spend it. John D. Rockefeller had a belief that "the power to make money is a gift from God." Both have created phenomenal wealth.

A person's beliefs can be heard in what they say. For that reason quotes are a great place to find beliefs. You can also ask yourself, what underlying assumptions about these people's capabilities and about the world are revealed through their statements?

Attitudes

What attitudes do the masters exhibit? Are they easygoing? Fun-loving? Friendly? Tough? Committed? Resilient? Frugal? Warren Buffett, Donald Trump, Bill Gates, and Richard Branson, all multibillionaires, have all been described as being obsessed with expansion and highly focused as a result. Trump, as well as Buffett, despises imbecility and incompetence. On the flip side of the coin, Buffett is well-known for his good-natured and fun-loving attitudes about life.

Memories

Find out what memories stayed with a person and had some overall effect on what direction he or she took. Not only is it fascinating, but this type of exploration allows you to see new possibilities that were previously hidden to you.

Trump once said that by the age of 16 he knew everything there was to know about building, without ever having taken a class. His father was a very successful builder, and Donald recalls following him from job site to job site soaking up information, which later provided him with the reference experiences to propel him to fame and fortune. This is also why Trump can rebuild so quickly when things go wrong. He's been there before so he knows how to recover based on his references. If you don't have the references to create what you want in your life, you've got to borrow other people's references.

At an early point in Oprah's career, she had the opportunity to visit Stephen Spielberg's production studio, Amblin Entertainment. Seeing this example of possibility expanded her references and she told herself she could create the same thing. This reference experience led her then to create Harpo Productions.

Decisions

Your decisions determine your destiny. In fact, in my modeling of extra-ordinary men and women throughout time, one thing I have discovered is that they really weren't extraordinary at all. They were simply ordinary people who made extraordinary decisions about the events in their lives.

When Nelson Mandela was in his teens, he was attending a traditional ceremony within his tribe that signified his passage into manhood. After the ceremony, one of the tribal elders stood up and said, "These are our young men. They are our pride and joy. They are our future. But the truth is that they are not men at all, and in fact they will never be men. Our land is not our own. They are second-class citizens in their own homeland. They are boys, not men, and they will always be boys." When Mandela heard those words, he made a decision to change the political face of South Africa. That decision changed his country and, ultimately, the world.

When Branson was young he was branded dyslexic. For many, that label would have served as an excuse for mediocrity and created a limiting decision about what was possible. Not Branson. He consciously decided at some point that the dyslexia didn't limit him but, rather, it made him more intuitive in business because he wasn't adept at reading financial reports. That is a very empowering decision to make about a condition that is usually considered limiting! Branson is not the only giant success to have been told he was dyslexic. So were Charles Schwab, Craig McCaw, Tom Cruise, and David Murdoch.

It is not the events in your life that shape your destiny, but the decisions you make about those events. Successful people's decision points can be found by examining the significant emotional events in their lives, and then looking at how those events became turning points. What conclusions did they draw from these events? And what direction did they take as a result? The answers to these questions will give you tremendous insight into their thinking—and into how much control you have over what you choose to make of your circumstances.

Language

What sort of language do your role models use? Are there any keywords that they use more than others? Master communicators use language to pull others into their vision and create momentum toward their future. For example, former President Bill Clinton used the word *we* 208 times in his final State of the Union address.

Warren Buffett recognized the importance of this factor in success when he said, "You should have a knowledge of how business operates and the language of business, some enthusiasm for the subject and qualities of temperament, which may be more important than IQ points. These will enable you to think independently and to avoid various forms of mass hysteria that infect the investment makers from time to time."

Meta Programs

The following 15 components of a cognitive profile all fall into the category of meta programs, which are overriding thought and behavior patterns individuals use differently in different situations. They are extremely useful in understanding how and why individuals do what they do, from making decisions and managing their time to prioritizing and leading.

Motivation Filter

This first meta program tells you what motivates the person you have chosen to model. Even a thought can be broken down into its six components: pictures, sounds, feelings, tastes, smells, and self-talk. Therefore, the question to ask when interviewing or studying them is, "When you think about your goals, are you making pictures, sounds, and feelings of what you want, or of what you *don't* want?" Their answer will reveal either toward or away-from motivation.

Here's a perfect example of what I'm talking about. I admire Oprah tremendously and she is an example that most everyone is familiar with, so she's a useful topic for illustration. She did an interview on America Online where she was asked what motivated her to work, and she responded, "to work or to work out?" The interviewer laughed, and Oprah continued: "If you want to know what motivates me to work, it's this: I am on a mission. You see, I feel that if I can assist people to take responsibility for their own lives, we can change the world. Now if you want to know what motivates me to work out, it's because I don't want to have a fat butt!"

Oprah was focused on a clear and powerful mission that compelled her forward. That toward motivation in her career produced consistently extraordinary results. The away-from motivation in her health and fitness routines produced inconsistent results. The first step to taking charge of your motivation direction is to set lofty toward goals. We teach in-depth methods for taking total control of your motivation direction in some of our seminars. However, recognition of the pattern is clearly the first step.

Orientation Filter

The person who is possibility oriented will think of all the possibilities in life, whereas the person who is necessity oriented may focus on his or her obligations and be moved to action by a desire to fulfill these obligations. Martin Luther King was someone who operated primarily based on the possibilities available until he became a reluctant hero and stepped up, out of obligation and necessity, to champion his cause. He later shifted back to possibilities, so King could be considered both possibility and necessity oriented. As you study the individuals you model, notice *why* they do what they do. It's possible to be possibility oriented in your thinking about one area of your life and necessity oriented in another.

Success Indicator Filter

Do the people you wish to model seek external verification of how they are doing? Or do they just know inside themselves whether they've succeeded or not? Are they more concerned with what others think about them, or with what they think about themselves?

The first thing Madonna used to do every morning was buy all the newspapers and magazines to see every item that had been written about her. If she didn't feel she was getting enough attention, she would do something to get herself back in the public eye. These actions show that she is or at least has been driven by an external success indicator. Warren Buffett, on the other hand, once said, "I keep an internal scoreboard. If I do something that others don't like but I feel good about, I'm happy. If others praise something I've done, but I'm not satisfied, I feel unhappy." Obviously, Buffett uses an internal success indicator.

Decision-Making Filter

This filter determines how people make a decision. Do they *see* something that convinces them, do they have to *hear* it, *read* about it, or *do* it? I've met managers who like to hear everyone's input first before making a policy decision. Others gather information from the Internet and periodicals, while still others just make a gut decision. Guess which filter Buffett uses—he once said, "In the end, I always believe my eyes rather than anything else."

Convincer Filter

How many options does someone have to look at or consider before being able to make a choice? For some people the decision is made immediately; some prefer to consider a couple of options; others require a certain period of time before they can make a decision; and some need to be consistently convinced even after they've made the choice.

When you examine someone like Richard Branson, it's very clear that he has an automatic convincer. He will jump into new business ventures simply because they appeal to his sense of adventure and they sound fun. He has tended to act on things without comparing options and to let those around him clean up any mess that is left in his wake, especially in his early days. Buffett can also appear to be automatically convinced because of his quick decision making. However, that's because his knowledge and experience have taught him to recognize the best deals. He's convinced of which stock to pick by looking at every option consistently and over a period of time. Buffett says that he doesn't look for seven-foot bars to jump over, but rather the one-foot bars he can step over.

Leadership Filter

Are your role models best at self-direction or delegating to others? Are they equally good at both? Or do they have no idea what they need to do, but can easily direct others?

Great leaders will more often than not be equally capable of leading self and others, like Branson. However, it is also possible for someone to be in a leadership position who hires the best people to play the role of director, while he or she simply becomes the figurehead. Generally, the most consistently successful people know what's best for themselves and others and can take charge of both. It's an important skill in any position of authority.

Energy Direction Filter

Have you ever noticed how some people tend to be extremely active all the time while others spend more time being reflective? The person who is at the far extreme of activity will take constant action toward their goals, whereas the reflective person will tend to do a detailed study of all the consequences of action before doing anything. And the inactive person simply reflects, but never acts.

Arnold Schwarzenegger said, "Seek out failure. The confidence and satisfaction of stepping over your supposed limit is enormous." The way he directed his energy puts him in the active category. Most successful entrepreneurs will tend to be very active in their approach to life, although they may learn from experience to reflect more before jumping in headfirst. Investors will tend to be more reflective but can learn from experience to be more active, as they train themselves to know and recognize value.

Performance Filter

This is different from the leadership filter in that it refers more to where people perform the best, and therefore gain their greatest pleasure.

Buffett demonstrated his independent and management performance style when he said, "My idea of a group decision is to look in the mirror." Celine Dion is an independent player, as was Elvis Presley, whereas their managers, Rene Angelil and Colonel Tom Parker, respectively, were management players. Where do the individuals you are modeling really shine?

Work Satisfaction Filter

Is the person more inclined to work with things, systems, or people? Donald Trump is interested primarily in working with things—the buildings he creates, the worldly trappings of success, and the deals he makes. The Dalai Lama gains satisfaction primarily working with people. Some politicians gain the same level of success but for different reasons—one senator might do what she does "for the people" and is great working *with* people, while the guy down the hall gets his job satisfaction from being part of the system and creating social systems that work. What are your role models most interested in working with?

Preferred Interest Filter

When people talk about what they do, are they more interested in the people they meet, the places they go, the activities they take part in, or the information they learn? This filter is made clear through an individual's words and descriptions of life and what he or she care about most.

Multibillionaire Ted Turner was very much an "activity" person throughout most of his life. When questioned early on about his priorities, he responded, "They are sailing, business, and family, in that order." While his priorities have shifted since then, looking at someone's preferred interests throughout the course of the individual's life can be quite revealing. Buffett's primary interest is in information and things. This provides him with the natural ability to recognize valuable businesses and make brilliant purchases.

Abstract/Specific Filter

Everyone grasps and assimilates information differently. The abstract thinker is the person who sees the big picture. Others have a great talent for understanding all the detailed workings of a plan. The entrepreneur is often an abstract thinker, as is the general in the armed forces. It is important for a leader to have the ability to move throughout the range of thought from abstract to specific.

Donald Trump has been quoted as stating, "If you're going to be thinking anyway, you might as well be thinking big." He grasps the big picture first, yet he is able to chunk down to the most minute details, such as the cost savings of putting only two hinges on each door rather than three when building a hotel.

Comparison Filter

This filter relates to whether people seek sameness or difference in their experience. Buffett is clearly a "sameness" person. He drinks the same Cherry Cokes day in and day out, he invests in companies he expects to hold on to for life, he even tends to stick with the same types of food. He once had lunch with Marshall Weinberg of the brokerage firm Gruntal and Co., who remarked, "He had an exceptional ham and cheese sandwich.

A few days later we were going out again. He said, 'Let's go back to that restaurant.' I said, 'But we were just there.' He said, 'Precisely, why take a risk with another place? We know exactly what we're going to get.' " This quality actually greatly contributes to his success because he looks for companies to perform at the same level or better over time.

Branson, on the other hand, falls more into the category of "difference with exceptions." He loves to launch many different businesses because the variety is important to him.

Challenge Response Filter

Do the individuals whom you want to model tend to deal with challenges with their head or their heart? Do their feelings dictate their business decisions or are they more dissociated in their approach? The other possibility is that under pressure they demonstrate the ability to use either or both. They can choose the most appropriate and effective response for the situation. Watching the clock run out on a close-scoring NBA game is fascinating because some coaches, although obviously feeling the pressure, will immediately go into level-headed straight-talking, while others will get more and more emotional. Both styles can motivate the team and get things accomplished. That's why it's valuable to know which approach works best when, and on whom.

The way to discover someone's challenge response is to simply observe the individual in a stressful situation. Notice his or her reactions.

Time Awareness Filter

Be looking for indications in your role models of whether they chart their schedule ahead of time or take each day as it comes. The through time person will tend to be punctual and carry a planner or just know in their head what they will be doing each hour of the day. The in time person, on the other hand, will be more interested in spontaneity. Such individuals have less direction and care more about fully experiencing the now. Again, using Buffett and Branson as perfect examples, they are through time and in time, respectively.

Focus Filter

This final meta program relates to whether people are primarily focused on themselves or other people. Are they self-absorbed or is their attention outwards? Mother Teresa was clearly others-oriented, while Madonna, at the far opposite of the extreme, has been self-oriented, especially in her early years. Ted Turner was very self-oriented early in life, then moved more in the direction of others later in life. What type of person will you want to emulate in this area?

Traits

You can often discover traits of masters by researching descriptions of how they interact with others and the world around them. Rupert Murdoch has been described throughout his life as being very inquisitive and having an insatiable appetite for learning more about those things important to his business. Celine Dion has been described as being extremely disciplined; she is possessed by her passion to perform. Madonna was often described during her rise to the top as being outspoken, brash, assertive, and willing to do anything to become a star. Sam Walton of WalMart fame had intense drive and competitiveness.

Skills and Skill Sets

Gandhi was a skilled communicator, as was Martin Luther King Jr. Barbra Streisand worked to develop her comic timing and became known for that in addition to her singing and acting talents. Richard Branson has tremendous leadership ability and is known for inspiring people to move toward a shared vision. Virtually every multibillionaire and activist I have studied has been an extraordinary salesperson. They are adept at selling their ideas, which you'll learn about in Step 3.

Once you've identified the skills and skill sets of the masters of the game, you can commit yourself to developing and perfecting those same skills and skill sets. This tells you exactly where to apply your energies.

Strategies

Strategies are the specific internal or external processes the masters do that allow them to arrive at certain results. There are three different types of strategies that you can enlist when doing inside modeling: micro, macro, and meta strategies.

Micro strategies are the exact order and sequence of steps that the master of a particular game runs through in order to produce a specific result. Most micro strategies will be run on an unconscious level within a matter of seconds. People have micro strategies for virtually everything that they do, including communicating, wealth, poverty, depression, learning, happiness, and so forth. Enlisting micro strategies can give you precise information about how to replicate a given result. I cover micro strategy techniques in depth in some of my trainings.

Macro strategies are primarily what you will be looking for after you have read this book. They are general things that someone does in order to produce a certain result. For example, if you examine the leadership strategies of Branson, you might find he does several things that, when emulated, could allow you to produce similar results. These include looking to make a difference through his companies, allowing people within his organization to constantly reinvent themselves in order to keep them engaged, and fostering an entrepreneurial mind-set within the people around him in order to get many great minds moving together toward the accomplishment of the corporate objectives. (I cover this particular leadership strategy in Part 3.) All of these activities would be considered macro strategies.

Finally, meta strategies are simply overall philosophies that cause individuals to choose all their other strategies. Meta strategies can be gleaned by paying attention to the master's driving force or highest value in life, as well as his or her philosophy about business or life in general. Nelson Mandela's meta strategy was to serve justice. Everything he did in life was to fulfill this purpose, even as he changed macro strategies along the way.

While micro and meta strategies are both important, macro strategies are where you will be placing most of your focus when you begin learning how to model. Be on the lookout for those things that your chosen role model does to create consistent results. For example, Rupert Murdoch manages his many companies by reading what he calls his "blue book" on a weekly basis. The blue book is simply a description of every financial inflow and outflow from each individual business. This allows him to keep his finger on the pulse of the entire organization and predict cash flow.

Bill Gates has had a consistent strategy of getting his products to market first, before any of his competitors, even if it meant sacrificing some quality. He would then use the general public as his quality control system by fixing software problems as they were reported. Buffett purchases companies with top-notch management already in place, rather than turning around companies that aren't working or building from the ground up. Trump has used a strategy of purchasing distressed properties when the owner has to sell and turning them into luxury properties under the Trump name. Arnold Schwarzenegger has had a strategy of seeking out mentors and then surpassing their achievements. Virtually every billionaire I have studied has a strategy of keeping an extremely tight lid on expenses while maximizing revenue. Many successful actors and actresses, including Oprah Winfrey, Matt Damon, Ben Affleck, and Pierce Brosnan, among others, started their own production companies rather than wait around to be cast in roles.

Schwarzenegger revealed one of his macro strategies for achievement when he was recently asked, in an interview in *Men's Journal*, "You've got money, fame, a great young family. Why take on governing the state of California? What drives you to constantly reinvent yourself even at this stage in your life?" Schwarzenegger responded, "It's not even really a matter of my choosing to make big changes in my life. It's like I get this vision without me controlling it of what I'm supposed to do next, and then that vision consumes me. It becomes me. And from the beginning I absolutely believe that I can do it, you know? It's almost like you have faith that you can do this thing and then you can't wait to get started on what you have to do to get there."

You should be getting a clearer picture of exactly what you will be looking for now to create a cognitive profile of each of your role models. The exciting process of Cognitive Reimprinting™ yourself for mega success begins with saturating your mind with new perspectives and knowledge.

Cognitive Reimprinting™

Jesus gave me the message,
Gandhi gave me the method.
— **Martin Luther King Jr.**

Prior to being imprisoned for 27 years on Robbin Island, Nelson Mandela played the extreme role of a radical activist. His role models had been revolutionaries and guerrilla leaders. While he was in prison he made a conscious choice to model himself after individuals who had impacted the world in more positive ways. He began to read books on individuals like Mahatma Gandhi. Eventually, through his actions and his vision of a free people, Mandela led a nation out of apartheid. He spoke of this vision in his Nobel Peace Prize address when he said:

> *The value of our shared reward will and must be measured by the joyful peace which will triumph, because the common humanity that bonds both black and white into one human race will have said to each one of us that we shall all live like the children of paradise.*

He went on to say, "We live with the hope that as she battles to remake herself, South Africa will be like a microcosm of the new world that is striving to be born." This conscious choice to model different leaders molded not only Mandela's values, but the entire nation around him.

Another powerful leader, Martin Luther King Jr., at an earlier stage in his personal crusade made a similar choice to emulate those who had transformed people before him. This process changed him, too, and then our world. It can do the same for you. Learning from others is an invaluable tool. It changed me and my life completely. It can do the same for you.

I formalized and accelerated this process as Cognitive Reimprinting™. It is based on my study of how change occurs quickly within the mind and what components of cognition specifically cause certain individuals to consistently achieve the results they do. Since we know that all thoughts and behaviors have corresponding neural pathways, Neurological Repatterning™ is the set of techniques that interrupt and eliminate existing thought and behavioral patterns to repattern in new neural pathways, while Cognitive Reimprinting™ completely saturates and neurologically reimprints the mind for preferred results.

Cognitive Reimprinting™ makes transformation occur more rapidly than ever. It begins with three major techniques: genius reading, mind mapping, and cognitive profiling. These are detailed in the pages that follow. There are two prerequisites to soaking in all the information you need. The first is to gather all the information. (You will choose later what you want to install and what won't serve you.) The second is to access a state of mind known as *expanded awareness.*

Gather Information

If you are unable to meet the person you wish to model face-to-face, the next best thing is to collect a body of knowledge about that individual and begin to extract the most pertinent information for mastering that particular game.

After you've figured out who you want to model, I recommend reading at least six books on each person, depending on availability. This will give you a complete picture and varied perspectives.

If your goal is to increase your wealth, for example, you might

choose one or more individuals who have amassed a fortune, prefer-
ably within your chosen field. If you have yet to decide what field is
important for you to make your mark in, then you may choose to simply focus on individuals who have produced most of the results that
you want, and let your vision of a chosen field develop as you expand
your references through the cognitive profiling process. The key here
is to listen to your heart and discover what sings to you most. If your
goal is to powerfully shape an organization or to move the hearts and
minds of the people around you, you may choose to begin collecting
books and other relevant information on people like Bill Gates or
Anita Roddick, creator of the Body Shop stores. If your goal is to find
nirvana and live in inner peace, collect books on those who have
achieved that goal. The sky is the limit. It's your world, so play the
game you want to play.

And remember that our goals are not exclusive. You might choose
to learn both the enlightenment strategies of the Dalai Lama and the
wealth-building strategies of Bill Gates. It's up to you. Right now you
are throwing your net wide to take in all you can to expand your realm
of possible outcomes.

Once you've amassed your body of knowledge on your chosen people, it's time to extract their rule books by getting into an optimal learning state.

Expanded Awareness

Expanded awareness is a state of mind that is also known as the learning
state, because it creates a mental condition of both total focus and recep-
tivity to new information. I detail the steps to being in expanded awareness on the following pages, so that you can rapidly increase the amount
of information you take in through your genius reading. Expanded
awareness is extremely effective for accelerated learning, as it will cause
you to be fully present in a state of what can be called *uptime awareness*.
While you are in expanded awareness, it is very difficult for the mind to
wander, which in turn causes a heightened state of focus.

There are two types of vision—foveal and peripheral. Foveal vision, also known as tunnel vision, is the act of focusing in on something

specific. Peripheral vision means looking at the wider or full picture, which is the realm of expanded awareness. The difference is depicted in Figure 8.1.

In the context of presenting, we have all seen people who are speaking to groups focus in on one single person for an entire presentation, to the exclusion of the group or classroom, yet they are addressing the group verbally. This is an example of foveal vision. In expanded awareness, you use your peripheral vision to cast your gaze over the entire group as if they were being addressed collectively or as one entity. Figure 8.2 depicts this distinction from another angle.

The easiest way to differentiate between foveal and peripheral vision is to do a simple exercise. Pick a spot on the wall somewhere above eye level. Stare at the spot exclusively and you will be using your foveal vision. Once you've done that for a few moments and experienced what it's like to be using only your foveal vision, the next step is

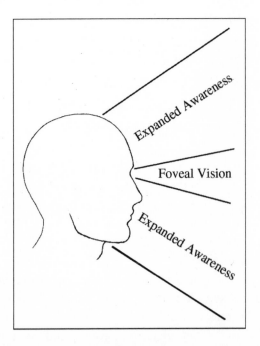

Figure 8.1   Foveal Vision and Expanded Awareness

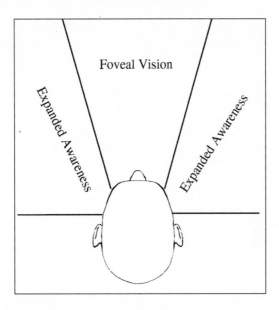

Figure 8.2   Shifting from Foveal Vision to Expanded Awareness

to continue looking at the spot, but begin to allow your vision to expand outward into the periphery. Notice that you can begin to take in whatever there is to see at each side of the spot. Allow your vision to expand as far outward to the sides as possible. While you're still looking at the spot, allow your awareness to begin to shift to the peripheral part of your vision.

Then, allow *all* of your awareness to be anchored in the peripheral while still looking at the spot on the wall. Place *all* of your attention in the peripheral.

Once you've experienced that, you can then bring your eyes down from the spot, but make sure that you keep *all* of your awareness in the peripheral. This seemingly simple technique will prove invaluable in your personal and professional development as you make it a habit to be in that state of expanded awareness.

Now that you have experienced being in this optimal learning state, it is time to get an overview of the basis of Cognitive Reimprinting™. This could be considered the downloading phase of installing new software for the mind.

Downloading Your Role Models' Cognitive Profiles

Let's first outline the necessary techniques of Cognitive Reimprinting™ and then examine each one more in depth.

A. Genius Reading—absorbing the most amount of information in the least amount of time
B. Mind Mapping—integrating this information in both the right and left brain
C. Cognitive Profiling—sorting and presenting it for conscious application

Genius Reading

The process of genius reading is the first major phase in reimprinting yourself to replicate others' success strategies. At this stage, your mind already begins to make new associative connections between you and your role models, expand possibility thinking, sort for ways to achieve your goals, and gain new reference points and knowledge. It requires the practice of expanded awareness so that all of this occurs more quickly and efficiently on both a conscious and an unconscious level.

Step 1: Center and Clarify Your Intention
Once you have chosen the books that will give you the vital information about the person you want to model, make sure that you are in an environment free of distractions. The key to effective genius reading is focus. Clear your mind and clarify your intention. In the case of extracting someone's hidden rule book, your intention is to identify the building blocks of that rule book. You'll want to discover all those internal filters that make their success inevitable, the specific values, beliefs, decisions and decision points, meta programs, strategies, traits, skills, attitudes, and so on. Clarifying your intention simply means being clear about what you

wish to gain from reading the book. This engages the reticular activating system, which will then sort for specific information. Direct your attention to the necessary information so you meet your objective or intention.

Step 2: Overview
The next step is to get an overview of the whole book. Start by reading normally the back cover and inside jacket of the book. Then read the table of contents and the introduction. Once you've done that, go into the expanded awareness state and rapidly take in the entire first page. It's best to do this in four seconds or less. Simply scan the page from top to bottom. Do not allow your eyes to focus on individual words, but rather both sides of the individual page and entire groups of words as you glide down the page. Then turn 20 pages or so and do the same thing with the 20th page. Continue through to the end of the book, rapidly scanning only every 20th page or so.

Your goal here is to get a sense of the author's style and the main concepts of the book. When you reach the end, rapidly read through the entire index and bibliography, again noticing any keywords that jump out or carry significant meaning.

All of step two can usually be accomplished in 15 minutes or less, depending on the length of the book. As you practice genius reading and begin to trust the process, you will find that your speed will increase significantly.

Step 3: Access Expanded Awareness to Absorb Two Pages at a Time
The next step is to go into expanded awareness and turn each page of the entire book rapidly. Although your eyes will rest somewhere in the blank center of both pages, your focus will be in the periphery so that unconsciously your brain registers every word on the page. Open to the first page and visually take in two pages without moving your eyes. It will be as if you are mentally photographing each set of two pages at once this time. Your peripheral vision should expand to the point where you can see the sides of each page as if looking at the entire picture of the open book. Do not concern yourself with consciously understanding what is written at this point. Simply trust that your unconscious mind is absorbing everything easily.

There are two things to keep in mind at this stage of the process:

rhythm and suggestions. You want to make sure that you continue turning the pages at a steady rhythm, pausing on each set of pages only long enough to take a mental snapshot of each set while in the learning state. While you are turning the pages rhythmically, you can also give yourself positive suggestions such as, "Relax. It's all going in, storing the material at the unconscious level. I'm getting everything and I'll recall it easily." You should be able to complete all of step three in 20 minutes or less, with your goal being to increase your speed. Trust the process. It may seem as if nothing is happening at first. A lot is happening. Remember, this is how the Reticular Activating System works, naturally sorting for relevant information. This is why setting your intention is so important.

Step 4: Access Expanded Awareness and Absorb One Page at a Time
Once you've mentally photographed the entire book, the next step is to go back into expanded awareness and go through the book again, this time a single page at a time. Part of what makes this process work is repetition. Repetition causes the information you are seeking to make a deeper impression at the unconscious level, and therefore increases retention and integration of the material. Start with the back cover again and rapidly scan down it. Then scan the inside jacket introduction, table of contents, and each page of the book. At this stage in the process you may find that certain components of the individual's rule book begin to present themselves to you. You may notice, for example, certain traits, beliefs, values, or strategies. As you notice these things you can slow down your scanning and make notes in the margins of the book. For example, if you were modeling Warren Buffett, you might find a section in the book where the author describes him as curious, in which case you could make a note in the margin that looks something like this: "*Trait—curiosity/How can I take on this same ferocious curiosity in my own life?"

It engages the brain further to add questions to anything you mark out in the margin. Because your mind responds to questions, your unconscious will work behind the scenes to come up with answers. Your mind is the most powerful computer that has ever existed, and if you ask the right questions, it will search for powerful solutions.

All of step four can be completed in 30 minutes or less when you are first learning. Once you have completed step four you may want to take a break, perhaps even overnight, to allow your unconscious mind to process the information and begin to make new connections.

Step 5: Speed-Read Line by Line

Speed-read the entire book again, this time line by line. Speed-reading is simply rapidly going through every line of the entire book starting with the back cover, table of contents, and each page in order, using your finger to guide you, if you like. You should be able to go through the entire book this way in the beginning in less than 40 minutes, always with the goal of increasing speed as you advance in your ability.

You may find that you have a sense of familiarity with the information because it is the fourth time that your unconscious mind is receiving it. In doing this, your brain has now been exposed to new ways of thinking and acting. In reading about the person you've chosen to model and specifically sorting for his or her hidden rule book, your imagination has been led in new ways. You've made new pictures, sounds, and feelings of these strategies, values, beliefs, and so forth, which has awakened your neurology by paving new neural pathways. You are now well on your way to integrating the information at both the conscious and the unconscious levels. The next step will continue to deepen those new synaptic pathways or thought patterns.

Mind Mapping

At this point you want to fully activate the right side of the brain and let the filter patterns reveal themselves through mind mapping. You will be extracting and integrating at the unconscious level all the important and applicable information you got from the books you read. This recall can be done after a single book or after reading two to three books. Mind mapping is a brilliant tool to create and deepen the new neurological connections and crystallize your newfound knowledge in both your conscious and unconscious mind. When you go through this process, you may surprise yourself with how much you remember and know already. Let's look at what is actually occurring inside your mind and body as you do this process.

The Neurological Effect of Mind Mapping

According to Dr. Paul Goodwin from Alaska Pacific University, there are $10^{10^{11}}$ (10 to the 10th to the 11th power) potential neurological connections in your entire body and mind, which is more than there are stars in the sky, more than there are grains of sand on the entire planet. This makes the brain redundant on a scale of 10 to 1 and the body on a scale of 3 to 1. What that means is that you have 10 times more neural connections in your brain than you will ever use, and three times more connections than what you are currently using in the rest of your entire nervous system. That's a whole lot of thinking potential in your mind and body. Your whole mind-body system consists mostly of a whole lot of neurological connections that haven't been fired off yet. Those $10^{10^{11}}$ connections could all potentially be transmitting information like a giant data-processing system, if we actually employed them. We don't employ them with our habitual thought processes. We do create more neural connections while mind mapping.

Whenever you have a thought or emotion or simply receive one of the millions of bits of information that assault your senses each moment of every day, an electrical impulse is fired off in your brain and is directed down a neural pathway. That means that every time you have a new thought or think of something in a new way, you establish a new neural pathway. When you are mind mapping, your brain is actually firing off new synapses, making new neurological connections, using more of its varied abilities than if you were just journaling or taking notes. The associative process of mind mapping literally mirrors the natural structure of your brain cells, as well as the brain itself. Several branches radiate out from a single branch connected to all others. You are accessing more of your own mind's potential by venturing down synaptic pathways as yet untraveled. Your mind map will resemble the brain cells depicted in Figure 8.3.

Habits are actualized neural networks. They are controlled by a specific sequence of neurons that form a finely grooved road. Once you go down that road once, it's easier to take it the next time because you don't have to use as much conscious effort, until eventually you have had that thought or experience enough times that it becomes completely unconscious. We hardly realize there is any other way to think.

Figure 8.3 Brain Cells in the Neural Network

As Tony Buzan describes the process in *The Mind Map Book*, "Every time you have a thought, the biochemical/electromagnetic resistance along the pathway carrying that thought is reduced . . . the more you repeat patterns or thoughts, the less resistance there is to them. . . . In other words, the more times a 'mental event' happens, the more likely it is to happen again."

A behavioral habit is then formed by traveling down only the synaptic pathways already created as the path of least resistance. That is what is happening when people feel stuck in their lives. They want to do or think one way but find that they keep falling back into old patterns. They only have that one option neurologically. Yet, if you took the same road to work day in and day out for 30 years, and then one day someone showed you a shortcut, it wouldn't take you long before you started using that shortcut. That is exactly what happens when you use mind mapping: You expand your brain's capacity, which creates new pathways, which then gives you new options and abilities to produce different results in your life.

The brain's cerebral cortex learns best by using a wider range of its skills. Optimal intelligence and mind-expansion occurs when we use all seven of them together. These seven skills are language, numbers, logic, rhythm, color, imagery, and spatial awareness. The reason mind mapping optimizes our learning and processing, our problem-solving, decision-making, and intelligence is because it uses every brain function simultaneously, as opposed to outlining ideas in a linear fashion, for example with a black pen on white lined paper. Mind mapping is a completely associative event, which takes advantage of the brain's intrinsic structure and how it naturally works—its function is associative, holistic, and tending to look for patterns and completion.

It has been proven that great minds like Einstein, da Vinci and even John F. Kennedy have indeed been great minds because they utilized more of this wider range of mental tools. This is what enabled them to achieve such great things and take us beyond where we had been before. They were accessing more of their brain's power by approaching the world in a more comprehensive manner. Mind mapping is an irreplaceable technique to activate the brain on all levels, fostering more creative thinking and imagination. It also augments the power to problem-solve, remember, get the bigger picture, and arrive at a solution, all necessary traits and skills of powerful leaders.

As you begin your mind map, you are integrating all the information you soaked in from the books you read. You are claiming that information as your own and bringing it into conscious awareness from the stores of your unconscious mind. This then activates those new behaviors, thought patterns, beliefs, values, and so on, directly into your nervous system. The institution of these new pathways creates new behavioral choices, and therefore new experiences. The more you stimulate those new neural connections with all this new information, the more deeply you are installing them, which will result in much more preferred experiences.

So now that you know why it's so powerful, let's find out how to create a mind map.

How to Create a Mind Map

You will need a large sheet of white paper and a dozen or so colored marker pens. The process will take about 30 minutes to complete. You don't want to be disturbed because you will be working from your right brain, which is the creative, free-flowing side of your brain. Interruptions will hamper your progress. So make sure you are relaxed and the phone is off the hook, the children are in bed, and no one wants anything from you for the next 30 minutes.

Start by drawing an oval or circle on the left side of a piece of paper, and put the name of the person you are modeling inside. Then draw two flowing lines that reach outward from both sides. These lines look like branching roots, and each should be a different color. Refer to the example in Figure 8.4 as you move through this process.

The two mind branches you have just drawn will be used to define the individual you are modeling in terms of two major categories. For example, you could write the word "Personality" on one branch and "History" on the other, or "Strategies" and "Values," depending on how you want to break down all the information you absorbed

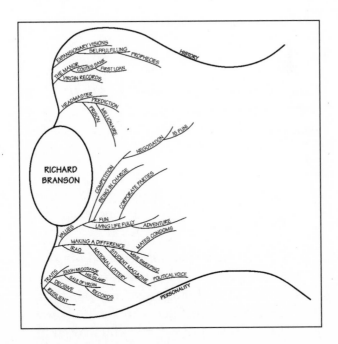

Figure 8.4   How to Create a Mind Map

from genius reading. Then you create branches that shoot off each wing. On each of the individual branches, you will put subcategories, whatever comes to mind. Put a maximum of three words on each branch. When you are creating subcategory branches, just let your mind run wild. Write down anything you can think of that relates to the book you just genius-read and the person you are modeling. There should be little conscious filtering at this point, just free association and creativity. Additional branches can shoot forth from each subcategory branch with additional subcategories.

When you mind map, you want to be in a flowing, creative state of mind. When you are starting to use this process it's a good idea not to concern yourself too much with coordinating colors with categories. In the beginning just allow yourself to associate freely and write down what you remember from the book. Once you become more familiar with using this technique, you can ensure that all values are a certain color, all traits are another color, and so forth.

Once you have gone through the process, your mind map may look something like any of the examples shown in Figures 8.5, 8.6, 8.7, and 8.8.

Cognitive Profiling

> *Employ your time in improving yourself by other men's writings so that you shall come easily by what others have labored hard for.*
>
> **—Socrates**

Now you are ready to translate all your collected knowledge and understanding for the left brain, which learns with more linear processing.

Categorize Your Psychological and Behavioral Map

Now that you have read somewhere between two and six books on the person you wish to model, and integrated your mind map, it's time to make a list of each of the major filter patterns of the individual being modeled. To illustrate this process, we will look at the profile of Richard Branson.

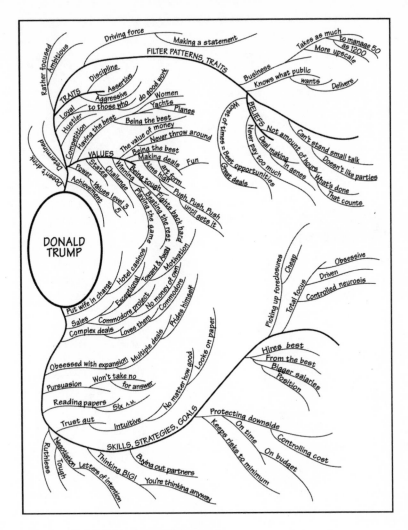

Figure 8.5 Mind Map of Donald Trump

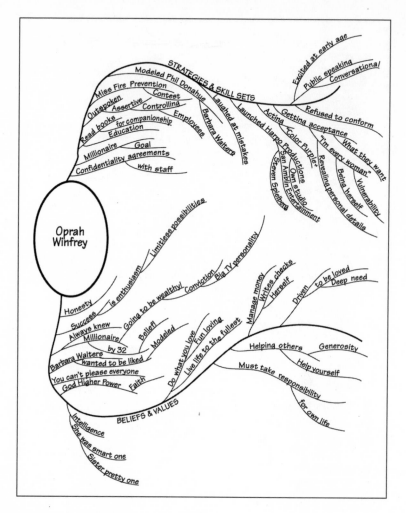

Figure 8.6 Mind Map of Oprah Winfrey

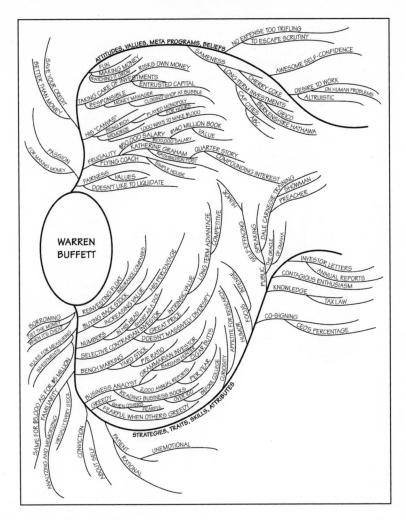

Figure 8.7 Mind Map of Warren Buffett

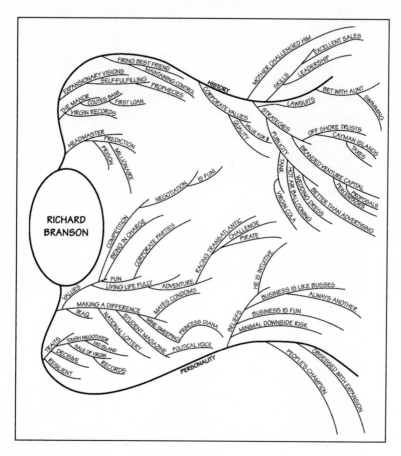

Figure 8.8   Mind Map of Richard Branson

Richard Branson's Cognitive Profile

Values

- Fun.
- Living life to the fullest.
- Challenge.
- Competition.
- Entrepreneurialism.
- Accomplishing "unachievable" goals.
- Standing out.
- Being the best.
- Teamwork.
- Making a difference.
- Frugality.

Beliefs

- Businesses are like busses—there's always another one coming along.
- Rules are made to be broken.
- Anything is possible.
- Negotiation is fun.
- Business is creative.
- Business is a way of life.
- If you go into business just to make money, you're in it for the wrong reasons; it must be creative.
- Every successful businessperson fails at some ventures.
- Business is fun.
- Personal relationships are vital in business.
- The way to handle a cash crisis is to expand, not contract.
- Take risks, be bold, but protect the downside.
- Needs partners in business to make up for his weaknesses.
- I control my destiny.

Attitudes

- Fun-loving.
- Adventurous.

- Life is meant to be enjoyed.
- Prepared to try anything.
- Live on the edge.
- Rebellious.
- Enthusiastic.
- Politically minded.
- Always looking to do anything he can to expand his businesses.
- Spends all his life working because he doesn't differentiate between work and private life.
- Cheeky, humorous.
- Thrives on opportunity.
- Curious.
- When told it can't be done, wants to prove them wrong.

Meta Programs

- Motivation filter: toward motivated.
- Orientation filter: possibility.
- Success indicator filter: internal.
- Decision-making filter: see and do.
- Convincer filter: automatic.
- Leadership filter: self and others.
- Energy direction filter: active.
- Performance filter: independent/management player.
- Work satisfaction filter: people.
- Preferred interest filter: activities.
- Abstract/specific filter: abstract to specific.
- Comparison filter: differences with similarities.
- Challenge response filter: choice.
- Time awareness filter: in time.
- Focus filter: self and others.

Language

- "Employees are first, customers second, shareholders third."
- "I don't think of work as work and play as play. It's all living."
- "It's much more fun in life being the underdog trying to topple Goliath. We've had a lot of fun trying to do things differently than the big established companies who've become a bit fat and

bloated . . . and overcharging the customer . . . and see if we can come in and do it in a way that we can be proud of." (The Biography Channel)

Decisions and Decision Points

- Early childhood experiences with dyslexia made him more intuitive as he couldn't understand numbers and math.
- Didn't do well in school and couldn't compete in sports, so he decided he would make his mark in business.

Memories and References

- Mother was always thinking of ways to make money.
- Brought up with attitude of putting other people first.
- Mother always wanted him to be busy, worked odd jobs, etc.
- Had the experience of being good at sports prior to his injury, so had a reference for excelling at something.
- When he left school at age 17, his headmaster predicted he would either go to prison or be a millionaire.

Traits

- Passionate.
- Determined to be the best.
- Ambitious.
- Resilient.
- Ruthless.
- Charming

Skills and Skill Sets

- Sales.
- Negotiation.
- The ability to persuade people to say yes.
- Never takes no for an answer.

Strategies

- Gets people to reinvent themselves in companies.
- Long-term financial growth strategies.
- Protects downside.

- Runs his companies out of houses.
- Has Virgin name registered as an offshore trust for tax purposes.
- Branded venture capital.

Armed with the inside story of what makes a particular person tick and what rule book he or she lives by, you expand your references and are able to adopt those traits to assist you in achieving your own success. With the cognitive profile, you have the internal and external road map for producing results far beyond your wildest dreams!

Now take a look at the skills and skill sets of the person for whom you have just created a cognitive profile. Make a list of the necessary skills you need to fulfill your brand of success. Rate yourself on a scale from 0 to 10 in terms of your level of expertise in each of those skills, with 0 being "no skill" and 10 being "excellent." Then commit yourself to becoming a 10 at each of those skills. Other aspects of personality can be changed through the Cognitive Reimprinting™ processes, but skills take time to develop. If you focus your energy and time on honing those skills like any athlete would in training, there will be nothing left to hold you back from rising to the top of your chosen field.

We have covered a great deal of territory up to this point in the book. You have been challenged to see that you create your own reality, and that what you create is dependent on a myriad of factors that shape your current life and your future destiny. You have become aware of all those aspects of your thought patterns and belief systems that control your behavior and, ultimately, your results. Now, you can either choose to be enslaved by them *or* you can harness all the power of your new perspective. You even have the tools to unearth your own hidden rule book, not only to understand yourself better, but to model excellence and change your own course forever. You have essentially downloaded all the mental software of the outrageously successful. The rest of the installation process takes place on even deeper levels at our seminars using more techniques for Neurological Repatterning™ that are difficult to present in a book.

Part 3 goes on to show you how to utilize your newfound power in concert with the most effective techniques of Creation Technologies™ to create a team that can ultimately win!

STEP

Play to Win!

YOUR
Dreams

Play to Win

Choose Your Game

Wake Up

CHAPTER

Magicians of the Material World

There are plenty of good ideas, if only they can be
backed with power and brought into reality.
—**Winston Churchill**

Whether you are playing cricket in Pakistan, soccer in Brazil, or baseball in America, certain skills and attitudes, exercises, and training systems have been developed for any player to achieve success, whatever the game. The game of life is no different. You must not only expand your emotional, mental, and physical fitness to perform optimally as a player, but also learn how to work optimally with your team to attain the ultimate prize—winning. Now that you have awakened to your internal filters and belief systems that have been determining your experience thus far, and you have chosen the game you want instead, it's time to train in all the skills that will make the biggest difference in moving you forward to your goal, and learn how to move forward powerfully with your team's support behind you. Whatever field you decide to play on, whether you want to be a CEO, an ingenious inventor, or a dedicated parent, just remember it is never a completely solo effort. This next section offers a compilation from my research of proven communication strategies, leadership skills, and character traits that can give you the edge you need to elicit the cooperation of others in the creation of your dreams.

When we look at individuals who have attained world recognition on a scale that seems larger than life, we tend to believe they just have a magic touch or they are special in some way that could never be explained. That is simply not true. From an outside perspective, a magician seems to be creating something out of nothing by pulling a rabbit out of a hat and the effect is dazzling. However, even magic can be broken down into practicable skill sets that become so innate they slip beneath anyone's conscious recognition. Yet, their effects are profoundly felt due to the end results that suddenly seem to appear out of nowhere. There exist several people whom I consider magicians of the material world. This last step is dedicated to learning the tricks of their trade.

Age of Communication

Success is not all about who has the latest communication technology, BlackBerry, laptop, or cell phone. In this age of communication, ultimate success is determined by who has the best communication skills. This means: (1) how and what we communicate to ourselves inside our own mind and body, which includes how we think; and (2) how we communicate with other people. Everything we have covered thus far has been about improving our internal communication. Much of the rest of this book is devoted to all the ways you can communicate with others to create synergistic relationships and inspire others to work together to carry your vision forth and make it a reality. The question is, how do you get 10, 20, 100, or even thousands of people conspiring for your success?

When Richard Branson was 15 years old he launched his first business venture, called *Student Magazine*. It was born out of frustration because he wasn't doing well in school. He had been branded dyslexic at an early age, so he concluded that school wasn't going to be the place where he would excel. Due to a knee injury he also realized that sports could not be his platform on which to shine. At this point he could have chosen to believe his problems were going to hold him back for the rest of his life—but he didn't. Instead he decided he'd make his impact in business.

He thought there was a niche in the market for a magazine that would air the political views of the student population in Britain, so he founded *Student Magazine*. In order to make it work, he had to sell ad space to fund the venture. In fact, at the beginning he had to sell ad space for a magazine that didn't actually exist. It's easy to look at him now, see his multibillion-dollar empire, and assume his level of success is out of reach for you. But Branson didn't build that empire overnight. It was a journey, and when you break it down, you realize that there were some simple, solid skill sets that went into making it happen.

So here he was, 15 years old, and he needed to sell ad space in a nonexistent magazine in order to make his vision a reality. He picked up the phone and started calling every business in town. There is a certain amount of courage that goes into that kind of action, as well as a level of communication excellence and negotiation skills, not to mention influence and persuasion. But there must also be an ability to convey a vision of something. Having the vision isn't enough. The magicians in the material world are those who can weave the abstract vision, then reach up into the ethers and pull it down with enough specificity to turn it into results.

Branson was able to do that and *Student Magazine* was born. It wasn't a huge financial success, so later in his career when the magazine started to flounder, he decided to use it to launch a little mail order record business called Virgin Records, and that worked a little better. But he was frustrated at the way the music industry worked because, as a retailer of music, his ability to make money was capped. He realized there would be more money in the business if he could get involved with the musicians themselves and actually cut the records rather than just sell and distribute them.

His next step was to create The Manor, a 15-bedroom house in the English countryside where artists could come and record music. This was an ambitious project; 15-bedroom country houses don't come cheap! Once again he found himself in a position where he had to communicate his dream and sell the vision, this time to investors.

Imagine a young kid in his early 20s walking into the bank and asking for a mortgage on a 15-bedroom house! Yet he did it. He walked into Couttes Bank and was able to communicate his vision for The Manor so successfully and so powerfully that he persuaded the bank to give him a mortgage.

He then persuaded his parents to kick in another $2,500 and his aunt another $7,500. Suddenly an idea had become a reality. Branson set up The Manor, which launched the Virgin empire we know today.

Warren Buffett, recently voted the most powerful man in the world by *Fortune* magazine, did the same thing. He is the most successful and richest investor of all time, with an approximate $36 billion net worth. When he was in his early 20s, he decided to create his first investment house. He studied what others had done before him, specifically Benjamin Graham. He modeled their methods, their performance, and their business, and decided to do the same thing himself. Yet he only had $100 of his own money, and investment houses required significantly more than that!

But Buffett had something far more valuable than money alone—he had vision and passion. He met with significant opposition, yet he was so passionate about his vision for the future that he managed to convince seven people to invest and eventually pulled together $105,000. This was a significant amount of money at the time, considering this was the early 1940s and he had no track record showing he could actually do what he was claiming he could. Nonetheless, he was able to powerfully convey his dream in such a way that he convinced seven people to believe in him. Getting others to collaborate in your vision is one of the essential keys to success on all levels.

Donald Trump is another one who has had to depend on his power of persuasion in countless challenging situations. Trump made his fortune buying distressed properties and turning them into luxury buildings with the Trump name on them. But when he first launched his early development ventures he did it with no track record and with little to no money of his own. One of his first development deals was the Commodore Hotel in New York City. When he announced his intentions, the people around him told him that he was crazy. This 28-year-old kid with no record of success wanted to renovate an old, seedy hotel and turn it into a luxury property during the height of the city's financial crisis in 1974. In order to pull this feat off, he had to use every communication tool and skill of persuasion in the book. He had to secure $45 million in loans. He had to convince the city to give him a huge tax break—to essentially become partners in the project by giving up their taxes—and convince Hyatt Hotels to partner with him as well, in order to pull the whole deal together. He convinced the people around him that his vision was worth investing in and would benefit everyone involved. Sure enough, he was right. Trump went on to make a fortune, as did they.

I look at all those stories and the results these people achieved, not just in terms of the money they made but in terms of the change they were able to affect in the world around them. These powerful individuals were able to act effectively in order to get results. They all thought outside the box of conventionality and then created outrageous dreams by selling these dreams first to themselves and then to those around them. That is my definition of power and influence.

As we travel through the last section of this book, I will share some of the specific techniques these great leaders and others like them have used to achieve their success. Taken singly they are powerful; used together they are exponentially so. Don't be fooled by the tools' relative simplicity. Sometimes when we start to talk about specific techniques, such as how to build rapport or how to be charismatic, we lose the value of the technique because our sights are on the technique and not on the result. This is akin to focusing on features rather than benefits in sales. The true benefit of learning this information is not in the techniques themselves, but rather the metamorphosis they are capable of producing. These techniques harness your powerful natural ability to influence yourself, your life, and those around you to achieve extraordinary results. Using and mastering the techniques translates into you becoming more magnetic, more charismatic, and consequently more powerful so that you can bring people together to create true win-win situations for all involved. You will be able to control and direct your own destiny and lead the hearts and minds of the people around you in such a way that you produce results a hundred times greater than you could on your own.

J. Paul Getty once said, "I'd rather have 1 percent of the effort of 100 men than 100 percent of my own efforts." At the time of his death, Getty was the richest man in the world and owned a controlling interest in Getty Oil and over 200 other companies. Through his foundation, he has funded museums and many other art and cultural institutions. He, too, knew the power of influence.

For me, the power of influence means the ability to create a vision in which you fully navigate the playing field of life and then enroll others in the synergistic pursuit of that vision to create a win-win scenario for everyone involved. The remainder of this book will explore in detail the skills and specific techniques to acquire those skills that you can employ to do just that.

Let the game begin!

10

Your Road Map to Success: Vision, Mission, Values, and Goals

*The ability to see and create the
future is the essence of leadership.*

—**The World Future Society**

The first step to navigating more of the playing field and producing results in your life is to get very clear on what you want. You have to begin taking conscious control of the goals you set. The more specifically defined your outcome is, the better your chances are of attaining it. Steps 1 and 2 have been about understanding why you are where you are and learning methods for expanding your playing field and changing your destination. The last step is working out where you would rather be and using powerful tools and techniques to get you there as quickly as possible.

I believe we are meant to celebrate the past and live fully in the now while consciously creating the future. It's now time to take charge and consciously create your future. How do you create something that's not right in front of you, in the same way that your present is? Begin by determining exactly what your own personal vision, mission, and goals are.

One of the best ways I have found to conceive of such a daunting

Figure 10.1 Your Road Map for Success

topic as navigating the playing field of pure potentiality—your future—is to think of your life as an extraordinary adventure or journey in which you are the hero on your way to fulfilling your ultimate vision. Figure 10.1 depicts this journey using four key symbols:

1. Sunrise = Vision. In the picture, the sunrise represents your vision, what you ultimately wish to achieve, as yet on the horizon. Whether you realize it or not, your unconscious mind has expectations of the future and, as quantum physics has proven, expectations rule outcomes. If you have no expectations, you have expectations of "no." The moment we bring our vision into our conscious awareness, it empowers us. The vision can be considered as the ultimate destination. Our vision statement at The Christopher Howard Companies was "by the year 2007, to empower over one million people to live wealthy and fulfilled lives." As this vision comes closer to fulfillment, we will write a new vision statement. A vision is far-reaching, yet can be revised along the way.

2. Path = Your Mission. The mission is the path that you take to get there and the specific means by which you accomplish that vision. Your mission comprises who you are going to be and what you are going to do to reach your vision. So, for example, in the case of The Christopher Howard Companies, our mission is "being the world's leading provider of resources for personal leadership and the expansion of human excellence."

3. Compass = Values. Your set of values is your compass. These are the things that keep you true to your path and true to yourself. You steer the course based on what you believe in, your ethics, and what is most important to you in life. Your compass is critical in getting you to your vision. Values are also very helpful when creating a team, because a team with shared values is extremely powerful. In some of our certification trainings we teach the process of aligning values within an organization, a couple, or any entity, because when people work together holding the same things as important to them, this generates stronger propulsion forward.

Those who work with me in The Christopher Howard Companies are all excited about what we do; we want to make a positive difference in other people's lives and have fun doing it. Integrity and pursuit of excellence are also important to me when hiring staff. Values can also shift over time. That is why my staff and I realign our company values together every year. The fact that we all have common values, which in turn create synergy and passion, makes me confident that together we will achieve the company vision at each stage of our growth. The same can be true for you, whether you want to transform your existing company, start a prosperous business, provide a happy, loving environment for your family, or create wealth for yourself.

4. Signposts = Goals. The signposts along the way are the individual goals or milestones that you set. They direct you to your final destination. They tell you when you've taken a wrong turn and guide you back to your path.

A business consultant friend of mine advises that people should set goals for themselves in three-month blocks. It's a highly effective way to manage your time and ensure that you are moving forward. A vision that may at first seem overwhelming can easily be broken down into three-month milestones that lead to its ultimate achievement. It has been said that most of us overestimate what we can do in one year's time and underestimate what we can do in a lifetime. Working in three-month blocks sharpens your focus and keeps you on track.

Take a few minutes now to think about what you really want for your life, and set your life vision and mission now. When you write these down in the space provided, they do not have to be definitive or perfect. This exercise is simply meant to provide you with a sense of direction. For the vision you can simply describe your imagined perfect day, one you would like to experience at some point in the future. It's remarkable that many people are prepared to spend hours watching TV, thinking about what to have for dinner, playing computer games, or surfing the Internet, yet they are reluctant to spend even a few minutes really thinking about their lives and what they hope to achieve. So please, I encourage you to stop for 10 minutes and take this first small step toward the future you want and deserve!

This powerful act alone gets your conscious and unconscious mind seeking more of those opportunities that are aligned with your purpose. It will also reinforce to you the fact that you are the only one creating your unique future. This realization can kick-start your future so you can finally begin to make your long-term goals a reality. Describe it in present-tense language but put a future date on it. You can write your vision for a 5-year, 10-year, or 20-year time frame. When you write your mission, simply describe the general path, the vehicle, or who you are going to be, such that it will lead you to the accomplishment of your vision.

Remember, your vision and mission may change over time, so

don't get caught up in trying to articulate them absolutely perfectly now. Review them on a yearly basis and rewrite them as they evolve, or as you find yourself getting clearer and clearer about what you want.

My Vision Is . . .

_____

_____

_____

_____

_____

My Mission Is . . .

_____

_____

_____

_____

_____

Once you've defined your vision and mission, you have identified the objectives of your personal game. Since completing Steps 1 and 2, you may notice that the parameters of what you now know is possible for your future are much expanded. Next, it's time to create your future and navigate the playing field by setting your goals. These specific goals will act as the signposts on your journey and will guide you toward your vision. They are your means of keeping score, or your way of seeing that you're on track. As you surpass each goal, you are building upon your confidence with each success.

The "What" Is Your Job, Not the "How"

It's never been about the money for me.
Money is just a convenient way of keeping score.
—Donald Trump

At this stage in the game, when setting goals for any area of your life, the most important question is what you want, not how you will accomplish it. You can figure that out later. Many people prevent themselves from achieving their dreams because they are too concerned with how they could possibly get from point A to point Z.

When John F. Kennedy said that man would walk on the moon within that decade, they hadn't even developed the technology to make that possible, and Kennedy himself certainly didn't know how that would happen. Yet he confidently expected it would happen, and on July 20, 1969, the first man stood on the moon. When Thomas Edison set out to create a working light bulb, he did not yet understand the "how." The light bulb was eventually created through countless trial-and-error efforts. As early as the 13th century, Roger Bacon said, "Cars can be made so that without animals they will move with unbelievable rapidity." It wasn't until 1769, about 500 years later, that the first working car was actually built.

The first step, therefore, is to ask yourself what you want—what, ideally, each step of the path should look like. You can't set a course if you don't know where you are going. Without knowing where you're going, you will end up like Alice in Wonderland, feeling lost, wandering without direction or purpose, and depending on others to tell you where to go.

> "Would you tell me, please, which way I ought to go from here?"
> "That depends a good deal on where you want to get to," said the *Cat.*
> "I don't much care where . . ." said *Alice.*
> "Then it doesn't matter which way you go," said the *Cat.*

Through your commitment to your vision and mission and through the goal setting you are about to do, you will have taken care of the "what." The "how" will reveal itself to you along the way.

How to See and C.R.E.A.T.E. Your Future

Now you are ready to C.R.E.A.T.E. your future the way you want it! This next powerful technique, called Strategic Visioning™, will give you the ability not only to see your future, but also to put goals in your future so that they actually occur. As management guru Peter Drucker says, "The best way to predict the future is to create it." The process of Strategic Visioning™ that will be described here is something that outstanding achievers do naturally, often without conscious awareness. I know several people, myself included, who use this technique at the beginning of every day or every week or before a particular event or meeting to affect its outcome. Once you learn the process, you can do it anytime you want with volition.

How you write down what you want is very, very important, so as you begin the first step of writing down your goals, make sure your outcomes meet the C.R.E.A.T.E. criteria:

C—Clear and concise

R—Realistic

E—Ecological

A—As if now

T—Timed and toward what you want

E—End step/evidence procedure

C—Clear and Concise

It is important that your goal be expressed in a clear-cut, unambiguous manner. It must be specific and concise. If you are writing a financial goal, for instance, use specific numbers. Specificity brings abstract concepts into reality. However, you also want your goal written as concisely as possible. A nutshell statement works best. When your goal is written in a nutshell, then your unconscious mind, which is the part of you that actualizes goals, can become impregnated with the idea and more easily focus all of its energies on how to accomplish it.

R—Realistic

Remember, we don't get what we want, we get what we expect. So it's important when writing short-term goals to set ones you expect you can achieve. Realistic means achievable to you. If you have never gotten what you want in your life, then scale your goals back by making them more attainable. If you have always gotten what you want, make your goals more grandiose—stretch yourself. Nothing breeds success like success, so it is important that you write goals that you really feel you can hit. A tremendous feeling of power comes with reaching the goals you set. This will breed within you that same empowerment to keep hitting your goals with accuracy and consistency. Once you've created your own track record of success, your expectation and confidence in your ability to succeed will expand, and you can stretch yourself accordingly.

E—Ecological

It is a good idea to run an ecology check on your goals, which simply means looking at the consequences of attaining that goal. Ask yourself, "Is this outcome safe for me, safe for others, and safe to the planet?" Or, "Is this outcome good for me, good for others, and good to the planet?" If you can say yes to all these questions, then you will know it is most likely a good goal to set, from an ecological standpoint. This thinking allows you to create win-win situations.

A—As if Now

The reason that we write goals in present tense is that once the mind has fully imagined something, it makes it far easier to accomplish. Because the unconscious mind doesn't know the difference between what is vividly imagined and what is real, when you visualize a goal as if it were happening in the present, it becomes much more compelling and achievable. So your goal must be written in present-tense language, as if you are achieving the last step right now in this moment.

T—Timed and Toward What You Want

Even though you are going to write your goals in present tense, you still must put a future date or time to your goal to indicate when you wish to achieve this outcome, even if it's tomorrow or later that same day. Otherwise it is likely to exist only in some vague future, in which case it might never actually occur. I've heard it said that a goal is a dream with a deadline.

The "T" in C.R.E.A.T.E. also stands for "toward what you want." It's important to express your goal positively, rather than including negative language about what you don't want. The unconscious mind cannot process a negative statement directly. If I were to say to you, "Don't think of a blue hot-air balloon soaring off into the sunset," you must first imagine it in order to then eliminate the picture from your mind. At best, it's a two-step process. So, for example, from a focus perspective you would not write, "I am not fat anymore." You would write, "I weigh 120 pounds and feel fantastic." Because your focus determines your results in life, you want to ensure that your words direct your focus toward what you want, not toward what you don't want.

E—End Step/Evidence Procedure

This is the piece that makes all the difference in this process, as opposed to general visualization. Always include the final end step that lets you know you've actually achieved your goal. This is the event, situation, or result that would have to occur in order for you to have attained your outcome. You can also think of this end step as your evidence procedure—how you are going to know when you have reached your desired goal. What is the last thing that needs to occur so that you know you attained it? For example, if you wanted to buy a home, you might write your end step as, "I am signing the papers on my new home," or "I have moved my furniture into my new home," or whatever specific picture you need to prove you have achieved your stated goal.

I was working with a car salesman who wanted to double his sales. So I asked him, "What's the end step, the last thing that has to happen so that you know you've doubled your sales?" He replied, "I'll be standing in the dealership looking up at the chart on the wall where they post our sales results. I'll see that I jumped from number 26 on the list up to number 1, and I'll see that I have X amount of gross sales next to my name." He brought the end step to a level of specificity that caused him to produce that result. Thirty days after our work together, the car salesman surpassed his goal, and one year later he was still at the top through consistent use of the Strategic Visioning™ technique.

A simple formula for verifying that a goal you are writing meets a majority of the preceding criteria is to use the format in Figure 10.2 when writing it.

For example, suppose your goal is to get a pay raise at work. You could write: "It is now November 22, 2005, at 5:00 P.M. I am standing in my boss's office, shaking her hand. She has just agreed to raise my income by 10 percent."

Once you've written the goal, verify that it meets all of the C.R.E.A.T.E. criteria:

- Your outcome is written in present tense with a future date. "It is now November 22, 2005."
- It is ecological. You've asked yourself if the goal is safe to all involved. Perhaps you've even determined that it's in the best interest of your company.
- You have a specific date for the accomplishment of your goal. Putting the exact time of day in there is optional. Include anything that makes it clearer to imagine.
- Your goal is stated positively. "She has just agreed to raise my income by 10 percent."
- Last and most important, you have included the end step or evidence procedure for your goal.

Remember, the end step or evidence is the last thing that has to happen so that you know for sure you have achieved your desired outcome. The end step in the preceding example is the boss shaking your hand, having

It is now _____ (future date)

I am/I have _____

_____

_____

_____ (end step/evidence procedure)

Figure 10.2   How to Write a Specific Goal

agreed upon the raise. The reason I used the word *income* instead of *salary* is that we don't always know how something is going to occur. It could be in the form of a raise, a bonus, stock options, and so on. The specific goal is a 10 percent increase of income, however that occurs.

Now that you understand the formula for writing goals, it's time to implement it. As you consider your vision in life, think of some intermediary steps along the way. Come up with a good two-week goal, one-month goal, and three-month goal that, which if you hit them, would move you closer toward your vision. Taking each goal, create your goal statements now and make sure they meet the C.R.E.A.T.E. criteria. Use the form in Figure 10.3 to complete this step.

1. It is now _____ (future date)

    I am/I have _____

    _____

    _____

    _____ (end step/evidence procedure)

2. It is now _____ (future date)

    I am/I have _____

    _____

    _____

    _____ (end step/evidence procedure)

3. It is now _____ (future date)

    I am/I have _____

    _____

    _____

    _____ (end step/evidence procedure)

Figure 10.3 Interim Goals

After writing your goals and checking that they meet the C.R.E.A.T.E. criteria, the next step in the process of Strategic Visioning™ is to set each goal into your future so that it becomes an accomplished fact.

The technique for putting a goal into your future time stream is one of the most powerful tools in existence for producing results in your life. It allows you to maintain a trajectory and move forward from goal to goal with precision and accuracy.

What Is Your Time Stream?

This [Theory of Relativity] required abandoning the idea that there is a universal quantity called time that all clocks would measure. Instead, everyone would have his or her own personal time.

—Stephen Hawking

Aristotle first spoke of the stream of time in *Physics IV*. Sir Isaac Newton described time in his *Principia Mathematica* in 1687, where he spoke of time as being like a single line or track that went on infinitely in both directions. Einstein added to our understanding of time even more when, in his theory of relativity, he abandoned the notion of absolute time in favor of the idea that each observer has his or her own conception of time. He proposed that time itself has a shape and is actually curved in some way. Today we know that people have a way of coding and storing their awareness of time in their minds and bodies which is spatial in nature. A standard psychological survey done in 1979, titled "How People Perceive Time," revealed that 99.9 percent of people have an idea of time that is spatially oriented in relation to their bodies. This is how you make the distinction between your memories of an event that happened yesterday and an event that happened 10 years ago.

If I were to ask you to stop for a moment and get a sense of where the past is for you in relation to your body, you might sense, feel, or even imagine that it is behind you, to one side or the other, inside you, or in some other direction in relation to your body. Do that now and point in the direction where you imagine your past is. There is no right or wrong answer, by the way. Whichever direction seems right to you is just perfect. Do not continue reading until you've pointed in some direction.

Once you've identified where the past seems to be, you can get an idea of where the future is. So once again, stop and ask your unconscious mind which direction the future is for you. It's simply a matter of trusting your intuition. In what area or direction do you imagine your future lies? Whatever direction you point is totally appropriate.

Once you have an idea of which way the past is and which way the future is, then imagine where your past and future are connected in a metaphorical line. Some people picture this line like a stream of time, a strip of film negatives, a chain, or a string. Notice that the past being in one direction and the future in another implies some sort of continuous line. Once again there are no wrong answers. Your time stream is perfect however you perceive it to be. I even had a client, an engineer from Boeing, who imagined his time stream as a flat, amorphous plane that circled around him.

Once you can imagine your time stream in your mind, the next step is to get acquainted with what it is like to rise above it. This entire process is done in your imagination. After all, Einstein did say, "Imagination is more important than knowledge." The greatest accomplishments and the greatest scientific discoveries of all time happened first in the imaginations of those who created them. Einstein himself created the theory of relativity by imagining himself sitting on the end of a light beam, traveling at the speed of light, and looking in a mirror at a clock behind him. He wondered, if he stayed at the front of the light beam, traveling slightly faster than the speed of light, would the clock stop or perhaps even go backwards? The imagination is powerful and can lead us to places we have never been before. So let's evoke the awesome power of your imagination and do a test drive above your time stream. First read the instructions once through, then set the book down in order to do the process. If exploring your awareness of time seems unfamiliar to you or as if nothing is happening, continue to trust your unconscious mind's ability to lead you. This exercises your mental flexibility and imaginative skills, both of which are qualities of the greatest leaders. The technique consists of four steps.

1. *Imagine rising above your stream of time.* Close your eyes and imagine that you can rise right out of your body and up into the air so that you are in the heavens above this current moment that we call "now." As you look down on now, notice that you can see yourself down below and that you can rise up higher and higher above your time stream. Rise so far up that when you look down on now, it seems very small and insignificant. Then observe your time stream stretched out in some sort of line, with the past going in one direction and the future in the other. At this point it's important to realize that this may not be merely a visual process. Be open to the possibility of experiencing the process as feelings and/or sounds, too. It's all in your imagination, one of the most powerful tools you have. As you imagine you are above the stream of time, the experience could be made up of pictures, feelings, sounds, or any combination of the three. However you imagine the process is fine.

2. *Imagine stepping back into the past, remaining above your time stream, as if you were up in the air or space, with the past down below you.* Once you have a sense of rising above the time stream below you, then simply take a step back into the past, all the while remaining above the time stream.

3. *Imagine stepping out into the future, remaining above your time stream, with the future down below you.* Now move from the past, remaining above your time stream, and step out into the future.

4. *Bring your focus back to now and back into the room.* Come back into the present moment, right where you are. This entire process should take one or two minutes. Go ahead and try it now . . .

Great. Now you are familiar with your own personal stream of time. This will help you immensely as you begin to learn to navigate your future.

Strategic Visioning™

Now let's look in depth at the Strategic Visioning™ process, then finish with a summary of the steps to put a goal into your future. Read this section through completely before doing the process.

The first thing to do is to read over the goal that you wrote according to the C.R.E.A.T.E. criteria. Then clearly imagine yourself at the end step, fully associated into how the achievement of that goal is going to feel, sound, and appear.

This is a key piece. Imagine stepping into that end step scenario. Engage your imagination so completely that you feel yourself experiencing that moment looking through your own eyes, not as a detached observer watching yourself from outside. See what you will see when you're at the end step and you have accomplished your outcome. As you do this, listen to the sounds around you when you have attained your goal, and feel the emotions connected with knowing that you can create whatever you want in your world. If you are not sure how to do this, just pretend that it has happened for real. We used to pretend as kids all the time so we know how to do it. You also do it every night when you dream. Once again, your brain does not know the difference between something that happened and something that you vividly imagine, so have fun with it and practice being a kid again.

Once you've stepped into the picture and fully experienced the feelings, it is time for you to adjust the sensory qualities of the scene. Imagine little knobs at the bottom of a television set. Begin to adjust the qualities like the brightness of the color. If it is a still picture, you can add movement. If it is moving, perhaps you can increase the speed. You want to adjust all of the qualities to intensify it or make it more real for you. What you are trying to create is a feeling of knowing in your own body that it's done. You can also adjust the sounds. Notice what you say to yourself when you've got your outcome. Maybe you just received that raise and you're saying to yourself, "Yes! I knew I could do it!" Finally, you can adjust the feelings that are present as well. You can just turn the internal emotions and external sensory experience right up, to increase the intensity of the feeling and experience—just like turning up the volume on the television set.

Having adjusted the scene to make it the most compelling for you, step back out of the picture, or dissociate, but leave your body in the picture, so that you see yourself inside the picture, kind of like a Polaroid snapshot of that end step.

This is the other crucial step. It makes the process far more powerfully compelling and exacting than simple affirmations or visualization. Most people who visualize their goals end their visualization while they're still inside the picture. With Strategic Visioning™, however, you step out of it so that you can see your body in it at that future time. This creates tension in your unconscious, like when you stretch a rubber band. This tension or heightened desire will pull you toward the goal. If you fail to do this step, your unconscious mind might feel convinced that you have already attained the goal, and therefore create no motivation to propel you toward it! Having experienced the gratification of the moment, your unconscious mind will begin to search for ways to make it happen.

Once you step out of the picture and can see yourself in it, take that snapshot in your mind's eye and then rise right up into the air above your time stream. When you've got the picture in your imagination and you are above your time stream, as if looking down from space, you will then energize the picture with all the life-force energy that it needs to become real. This is done by breathing your life essence into the picture.

This part of the process may seem a bit esoteric to some people but it is very important, so please just trust the process. You are focusing all of your will or intention on making this happen. Simply imagine that you are holding the picture in your hands, if you want, or in your mind's eye, as you remain above your time stream now and inhale. Then exhale through your mouth, making a "ha" sound and blowing life-force energy into the picture. Do this three times.

When you have fully energized the picture, you can then step right out into the future above the time stream until you arrive at a position right above the date where you said this event would occur. Trust that you will know where that is—go with your instincts. When you arrive above that date, simply drop the picture right down into the time stream and allow it to take its place there, as if your word were law in the universe. Once you notice that the event has taken its place in the time stream, then turn and look back toward the past; notice that all of the events in your time stream reconfigure themselves to support this outcome. Everything that had to happen in order for this event to occur shifts into place rapidly and unconsciously within the time stream in order to lead naturally to the occurrence of your goal.

Lastly, look off toward the future and notice that all of the events in the future also reconfigure themselves in light of this event. This event becomes a cause set in motion that changes your entire future as well. Once you've observed that, come all the way back to now and back into the room.

To help you remember these 11 steps, here is a summary of them:

1. Get the end step of your goal in mind.
2. Associate into the end step. Engage yourself in it, so that you are looking through your own eyes.
3. Adjust the qualities of the scene or the internal representation until you have a feeling of reality.
4. Step out of the picture. Dissociate, so that you see your body in the picture.
5. Take this picture and rise above the stream of time.
6. Energize the picture with three breaths.
7. Move out into the future to a place right above the future date.
8. Drop the picture down into your time stream, into the date you specified.
9. Notice how events reconfigure themselves in your time stream to support the goal.
10. Notice the future reconfigures as well.
11. Come back to now.

While this process may seem very simple, and perhaps even a little silly, I promise you it is the same process I used to turn my life around many years ago and continue to use today. The results you will achieve using this technique will amaze you. We limit our power to create success when we underestimate the unconscious mind's tremendous capabilities and rely for results solely on the conscious mind and will, which constitute a mere 10 percent of the brain's capacity. Utilize the other 90 percent. Consistent use of the process to achieve all your set goals will turn you into a master navigator of the playing field of life.

Once the goal is written, it shouldn't take more than a few minutes to do the entire visioning process. I use it before doing anything in which I have a significant investment in the end result. I once taught the process to a car salesman, who got so good at using it that he told me he could actually put into his future the name of the person who would buy a car from him each day, even without having met that person yet, and someone with that name would show up and purchase a vehicle.

Another woman from one of my seminar programs put a relationship into her future with a man named Thomas whom she had never met. Within three months he showed up in her life. Another woman was living in a trailer park, and after putting a new home in her future, one of her clients actually bought a house for her. It is an incredibly powerful process, so please don't underestimate it. Don't brush over it because you think you've tried something similar and it didn't work. Strategic Visioning™ has distinctions that make it highly efficient and productive. Use it now. You will be astonished at the speed with which you start to see your desired results.

11

The Success Formula of Masters

Even if you're on the right track,
you'll get run over if you just sit there.

—Will Rogers

After years of extensive research into what the world's legends of wealth and power have in common, I discovered what I consider the success formula of the masters. It is a kind of impeccable success strategy or pattern of habitual behaviors that invariably turn a dream into a reality. Here are the five major keys to realizing your dreams:

1. Put the goal into your future (Strategic Visioning™).
2. Take immediate action.
3. Have enough sensory acuity to know whether you are being effective and enough flexibility to adjust your behavior until you produce the results you want.
4. Utilize everything that occurs to your advantage.
5. Operate from a physiology and psychology of excellence.

Let's go over each of them separately.
First, put the goal into your future. Even if the masters never per-

129

formed the formalized process of Strategic Visioning™ as you just did, putting goals into the future is an important part of the master strategy utilized by all successful people, whether by Thomas Edison, who created the light bulb; Oprah Winfrey, who created the number one talk show in television history; Rupert Murdoch, who launched News Corporation; or Nelson Mandela, who helped to liberate a nation. Imagining a specific goal happening is the point at which the person becomes possessed by passion.

Being passionate is the number one trait the mega successful share. However, it is a difficult quality to describe. People just know it when they feel it. Passion usually takes over and provides the necessary impetus and fuel for success when you have a purpose that is aligned with your values. That is why I had you get very clear about what game you most want to play, then put your goals into your future. That will continue to provide the passion to get you through any challenge. The rest is learnable.

Second, take immediate action. Despite what some well-meaning people say, attaining exactly what we want in our lives is not only about thinking positively. Once you've set your outcome, you've got to do something about it. Maybe you've heard of the husband lounging on the sofa, who said to his wife, "I'll think about digging the garden in a little while. Right now I'm thinking about painting the screens." Thinking about painting the screens is still no substitute for painting the screens.

Someone who was attending one of my seminars approached me once and said, "I'm having trouble creating what I want in my business. I've been to all kinds of seminars and I've really got my thinking straight, but I'm still waiting for it to manifest in my life." I said, "Well, I've always been good at manifestation, but I've never waited for it."

You've got to act!

Do *something*—anything! Thought alone will not create the result you want. Even a well-laid plan is not enough. You have to put feet to your dreams. Take baby steps if you need to. But just realize, people with massive wealth are people who take massive action.

The way to produce effective and efficient action is to simply apply the third key in the success formula for masters until the result is achieved. That is, have enough awareness and sensory acuity to know whether your actions are effective and have the flexibility to adjust your course until you produce the results you want. Sensory acuity is the ability to assess whether you are getting the results you want. They say the definition of insanity is to do the same thing over and over again and expect a different result. Sensory acuity is having the awareness to monitor the results and make the necessary adjustments so as to fine-tune your actions to ultimately achieve your desired result. You may have to adjust your course slightly as you go, and if you stay on course you will arrive at your destination.

If a pilot takes off from New York to fly to Dallas, he or she may be technically off course several times during the flight. By monitoring the appropriate situation, remaining aware of the flight path and the relevant dials, the pilot is able to take appropriate, effective action to get back on course and land safely at his intended destination.

The fourth major factor that will launch your game to the next level is to utilize everything that occurs to your advantage. Once you have set your goals in place you will undoubtedly experience what most consider obstacles. They mistakenly interpret them as barriers to reaching those goals. The people who are the most successful in life are masters of utilization. John D. Rockefeller once said, "I always tried to turn every disaster into an opportunity." The crucial difference between those who live from paycheck to paycheck and those who hop from vacation resort to vacation resort is their interpretation of and response to obstacles.

The moment we set a goal, we create our own obstacles. Think about it. Before we decide on a goal, there are no obstacles to its accomplishment. For example, say you wanted to attend one of my programs. Once you have set the goal, you may find that there are some obstacles that arise. You may say "I don't have the money," or "I have other obligations that weekend," or "I don't know how I will get there." None of these considerations were relevant until you created the goal to come to the seminar. Your other obligations may already have been relevant to you, but only became an obstacle when the possibility of a conflict arose because you wanted to come to the weekend seminar.

The easiest way to avoid obstacles is to have no goals. This is why many people don't even bother setting goals in the first place; they don't want to deal with the obstacles to a goal's accomplishment. The moment we set a goal, the moment we choose the direction, the obstacles become real. Every time you run into an obstacle in the future, you will understand that the very fact that you hit the obstacle means that you are on course to your goal. Then all you need to do is find a way to use that obstacle to your advantage. Have enough behavioral flexibility to think about your situation differently. You may need to take a detour to get around the obstacle, but often these detours are necessary to the journey. So persist. Obstacles are just life's tests to see how badly you want the goal in the first place!

Donald Trump attended the grand opening of a golf course that he had purchased in Southern California. As it began to rain, a reporter asked him, "Aren't you upset that it's raining on your opening day?" to which he replied, "Are you kidding? Rain on the opening day always means good luck and success!" He used the circumstances of the moment to his advantage and chose the meaning to support his outcome.

When Richard Branson was still a teenager and his *Student Magazine* wasn't making money, he used the situation to his advantage by launching a mail-order record business through the magazine. The mail order record business was a little company he called Virgin Records. Later, when the mail carriers went on strike and the strike threatened to put his business under, rather than give up, he opened a storefront, which became the first Virgin Records store! This use of circumstances and his willingness to see a different route launched him on a path toward extraordinary financial success.

These abilities can also be applied when making corporate decisions. The best companies in the world use this strategy for success. When Pfizer pharmaceuticals was developing Viagra, their expectation was that it would treat chest pains. When it didn't work, they almost scrapped the entire project. If the researchers and executives had not been able to think beyond their original intentions, they would never have opened up a whole new market, offering new life to an entire population of men and women. The revenues from this supposedly failed experiment were $788 million within the first nine months it was on the market. Viagra far surpassed sales of Prozac as the most successful drug ever launched. These are two prime examples of how utilizing sensory acuity and behavioral flexibility determined these individuals' choices to turn seeming obstacles into opportunities for further expansion.

And finally, operate from a physiology and psychology of excellence. Physiology is important because you must hold yourself in a way that is congruent to your vision. Your physiology must match your statement. You couldn't, for example, be smoking as you announced to the world the imminent launch of a new chain of fitness centers. Similarly, you couldn't meekly suggest that a new product you developed is going to change the planet. You have to stand up for what you believe in and put yourself on the line to achieve it. The psychology of excellence is also very important, and again it's about being congruent with your vision and being confident enough to stand up for what you believe in to make it happen.

One of the most important things I have learned is to keep moving confidently forward toward my long-term vision no matter what happens and to be kind to myself along the way. If I had beaten myself up each time I didn't hit a goal right on, I would have quit a long time ago. As soon as I set out on my current career path, I set a goal for the first year to make a million dollars in personal income. I also set goals to be speaking and teaching seminars all over the country within that year, to have a best-selling book, and to be the leading authority in my field. None of those things happened. But what did happen was that I set myself in a direction that was to become my life's purpose. Although I didn't even come close to my goals that first year, I did make headway. I was teaching seminars in a few different places around the country. I was becoming an expert in my field. Did I beat myself up? No way! I said, "Good job, Chris!" and kept going.

Remember that most people overestimate what they can accomplish in one year's time and underestimate what they can accomplish in a lifetime. This turned out to be very true for me. Within two years of setting my original goals I really was speaking all over the country. Within two and half years I was finally writing my book. Within four years I was speaking internationally. Was this a failure? Not even close. It was a major victory! Keep your eye on the big picture and your long-term vision, no matter what.

I remember when I was organizing one of my very first seminars years ago, I ended up canceling it because, as far as I was concerned, not enough people had signed up. A friend of mine said, "Well, you gave the seminar business a shot, what are you going to do now?" Even though I was really upset at the time, I smiled to myself about that defeatist kind of thinking. I would never even consider giving up the way he had suggested. Today it's not unusual for our seminars to sell out completely. The people who succeed in life realize that there is no such thing as failure. Take everything as feedback, because feedback is the breakfast of champions. Maintain the congruence of your physiology and psychology of excellence knowing your own success is inevitable. It will get you everywhere.

12

CHAPTER

Who Is on My Team?

*You can have the most beautiful dream in
the world, but it takes people to build it.*

—**Walt Disney**

You have clarified your vision and established a mission for how you are going to bring it into manifestation. We've discussed how to set up the signposts along the way and the master strategy for success that underpins everything that master manifesters do. The next step is enrolling others in your vision so you can create leverage and achieve outstanding results. Your team members provide power for your good ideas that can help you translate your vision into reality. How do you produce the fuel that will compel your teammates to drive you powerfully toward your vision? The fuel is created by helping them to achieve their deepest desires—by helping others to self-actualize. By helping enough people to get what they want most, you certainly will get what you want most.

First think about who you want on your team as you move toward your objectives. Napoleon Hill, author of *Think and Grow Rich*, one of the timeless classics in personal development, talks about the mastermind alliance—creating synergy and attracting people to you who will assist in the accomplishment of those goals.

Take a moment now to think of six people, either actual individuals or roles that you will need someone to fill in order for you to achieve your goals. Write down the name of a person if you know of someone appropriate, and why that individual is important to the accomplishment of your vision. If you don't know someone specifically, write down the role and why it is important. You'll be surprised at how quickly the world will conspire toward your success when you get clear about what you need. Next week you might just bump into a person that can do exactly what you require.

My Team   *How They Will Benefit*

1. _____   _____

2. _____   _____

3. _____   _____

4. _____   _____

5. _____   _____

6. _____   _____

Once you've named those people or those roles, make a list of the advantages they would gain by getting involved in your dream. What's in it for them? How is what you want going to also assist them in attaining what they want? If you don't know the people on your list yet, or if you need a kick-start to help you discover how they might be able to benefit through the accomplishment of your vision, you can just imagine yourself rising out of your own body and down into theirs, and imagine you are looking out through their eyes. How could that person benefit from assisting you in your dream? What is important to them? How would they best self-actualize?

Once you have begun to identify the major players on your team, your goal then becomes learning how best to work in concert with your team in order to win the game together. This is accomplished first with intention and second through communication. The questions you want to constantly be asking yourself are, "How can I assist them to self-actualize through the accomplishment of my vision? How can I help them get what they want most?" Then, through your mastery of communication skills, as presented here in Part 3 of this book, you will be able to maneuver on the playing field with many players working in concert toward the same goals.

Of vital importance to you in captivating your team are your sensory acuity and rapport-building skills. Master communicators who get others to take action always employ sensory acuity. When pulling together a team, sensory acuity is the act of being aware enough to pick up on the various signals that people give you as you talk to them. Are you really getting through to them or not? The answer lets you know how to adjust your communication to make sure you are being understood. Have you captured their imaginations or not? Are you connecting to this person or not? This is such an important issue for enrolling others into your vision that we will further discuss some of the ways you can fine-tune your sensory acuity.

The Importance of Sensory Acuity

Freud once said, "He that has eyes to see and ears to hear may convince himself that no mortal can keep a secret. If his lips are silent, he chatters with his fingertips, betrayal oozes out of him at every pore." He was referring to the fact that we are always communicating something, even when we are not using words. People who are outstanding communicators are able to notice things in their sensory awareness that others do not. They are aware of the minutest shifts in the person they are communicating with or even in an audience, and can adjust their communication accordingly to ensure the message is getting through. To develop your ability to notice things that most people don't even realize exist will unlock your potential to create the results you desire in your interpersonal communications.

How would you like a way to know whether your communication is getting through to someone or not? What if you could notice from moment to moment where your communication was going with someone so that you could change it, if necessary, to produce exactly the result that you wanted? Sharpened sensory acuity will allow you to do these things and more.

Hallucination versus Sensory Feedback

The key to using sensory acuity is to refrain from attributing any particular positive or negative meaning to any of the physical reactions you perceive. There is a difference between sensory feedback and hallucination. I remember being in a meeting once with my partner. We were interviewing a particular prospect we were considering hiring for a very important position within the company. When I asked the prospect a question regarding her previous job, her face completely flushed and her lips tightened. I didn't try to mind-read or, as I refer to it, "hallucinate" what emotion the question triggered. It could have been anything from a reminder of a love interest to an argument or an unresolved situation that she still had resentment about. The response only indicated to me that there was something there that I could choose to delve into further or inquire about later. But it was information, nonetheless. During crucial hiring decisions that can make or hurt a company, the more information gathered the better.

Our purpose in this section is simply to become aware of this more subtle level of communication delivered through the minute changes that occur in those we communicate with from moment to moment. You needn't guess what they are thinking or what's going on inside of them. Instead, simply realize that something in their physiology, tonality, or energy has changed. These are a few things to look out for that indicate there is an emotional response occurring beneath the surface:

- *Pupil dilation:* A person's pupils will change from smaller to larger as they dilate.
- *Lower lip size:* The lower lip of an individual will actually change from thinner to fuller. The easiest way to tell the difference is the appearance of lines on the lip when it is full and a stretched smoothness when it is not.
- *Skin tone:* Skin tone can go from tight to relaxed. This can be noticed by looking at how shiny the skin is; the tighter the skin, the more shine there will typically be.
- *Skin color:* Skin color can range from lighter to darker, or from pasty to flushed.

- *Breathing location:* The breathing location of an individual will vary from moment to moment. It can range from high in the chest to low in the belly.
- *Breathing rate:* The person may breathe faster or slower in a given moment.
- *Muscle movement:* Minute muscle movements can also be noticed, and they have the potential of telling us much about the effect of our communication.

You might be wondering at this moment, "Who cares? What difference could this possibly make in my leadership abilities?" The reason these external indicators are important is that they indicate a change in internal state. Calibration is taking one set of distinctions and comparing it to a second set of distinctions. Once you can do this, you can tailor your communication from moment to moment for maximum impact.

For example, I had a client who visited me because he was a procrastinator. He told me that he just couldn't get moving and wasn't excited about life anymore. So I talked to him for a while and noticed what he was like when he talked about his life. He seemed very lackluster and unenthusiastic. Then I asked him what got him excited in life, what inspired him. He began to talk about his love for waterskiing. The activity itself wasn't as important as the state that he went into when he spoke about it. I noticed that when he started to talk, there was a micro muscle movement at the side of his neck, like a twitching.

My client was currently filling a lesser, non-engaged role in the company he worked for, so I started talking to him about the possibility of becoming a sales manager there, and he wasn't inspired by that. I then used an analogy (very powerful, and I'll talk about how to do it in Chapter 17) to illustrate my point and see if I could get him to see the possibility. His father had been in the military, so I said, "It's kind of like being the general instead of the foot soldier." We talked about that for a while, and through this analogy he started to see the big picture. As soon as that happened, I noticed this micro muscle movement again. I was able to use this to monitor whether my communication was actually getting through to him, because I had developed my sensory acuity skills enough to notice the shifts in calibration. Along with the micro muscle movement, there were also changes in skin color and pupil dilation, which only served to verify something occurring beneath the surface; in this case, inspiration.

By mastering sensory acuity, you become aware of things that most people are not aware of, things that can provide incredibly useful information in all walks of life, from a business negotiation to a romantic relationship. A word of warning, however: *Avoid attaching meaning to the change.* Sensory acuity is valuable in that you can become aware *of the change*, and then you can start to see a correlation between that change and an emotional response. For example, with my procrastinating friend, I had no idea what the twitching muscle meant until I had spoken to him for a little while and noticed the correlation between the minute muscle movement and his being excited. That same movement may mean something completely different in someone else, so don't start to categorize things as good or bad. Just notice the difference and look for connections that can give you a clue to the meaning for that person. Being aware enough—and taking the *time* to be aware—is a very powerful tool and can assist in the deepening of rapport, which I discuss next.

13

CHAPTER

The Power of Rapport

Anything is possible in the presence of a good rapport.
—Milton Erickson

When you look at the most charismatic leaders, you'll notice one of the most fundamental skills they have in common: the ability to create instantaneous rapport with anyone. Rapport is a deep and unconscious connection to another person, a feeling that you have a lot in common with them. When developing rapport, you are not necessarily getting a person to like you; you are creating an atmosphere where they will recognize that you are alike. This allows them to warm to you, accept you, and trust you more readily. Good rapport fosters understanding and, contrary to popular belief, it is a skill that can be learned. The ability to create rapport is the foundation of great communication and outstanding leadership.

There are two underlying principles of rapport. The first is that when people are similar they tend to like each other. The second is that there are levels of communication beyond the words you use.

In 1970, anthropologist Ray L. Birdwhistell, who devoted his entire research career to the study of human communications, wrote the book *Kinesics and Context*. In this book, Dr. Birdwhistell explains that the effect of our communication is less dependent upon words then one might think. In fact, his research revealed that 55 percent of the effectiveness of any communication is due to the physiology of an individual, whereas 38 percent is a result of the vocal tonality, and only 7 percent is a result of the actual words. In the context of becoming an effective leader, you need to develop each aspect of communication to get a message across, especially physiology and tonality.

Physiology

Physiology refers to what you are doing with your body. It is the first impression that someone gets and it has an enormous impact on what you are communicating to the world. Your senses are literally being bombarded with information that is being processed so fast you're not even aware of it. This is why physiology is such a huge influence on communication, because it occurs before you even open your mouth.

What does your physiology say about you? I'm not talking about just your body shape and what you wear. I'm talking about how you hold yourself. Do you look the world straight in the eyes, or do you slouch and scuffle around? Do you walk with purpose or amble to your destination? Do you project an air of confidence or trepidation?

How we move is often indicative of how we feel, and how we feel will very often determine what we do and how people perceive us. There is a set pattern of movement and breathing that is required in order to do "unhappy." Physiology affects and even creates emotional states and vice versa. Unhappiness is more than just a thought. It is something you communicate to your own body so that it can behave in an unhappy manner.

Anyone can learn how to do "depressed," so why wouldn't you also be able to learn how to do happiness or confidence? You can. It's all a matter of communicating those states to your body and having your body respond with the appropriate mannerisms. Conversely, you can take on the postures and facial expressions of a state such as happiness and notice how it affects your internal state too.

Tonality

Tonality is one of these seemingly minor factors that, on the surface, don't seem to have much impact. Surely what you say is what you say, and that's all there is to it, right? Wrong. Do the next little exercise and you will understand the power of tonality.

Read the following sentence out loud without any emphasis on any word.

"I never said he stole money."

Now read the same sentence out aloud again, but put the emphasis on the italicized word.

"*I* never said he stole money."

"I *never* said he stole money."

"I never *said* he stole money."

"I never said *he* stole money."

"I never said he *stole* money."

"I never said he stole *money*."

This is exactly the same sentence, with exactly the same words, in exactly the same word order, yet the shift in emphasis dramatically changes the meaning. You can see, or rather hear, the importance of tonality to convey a vision.

Words

Most languages have a huge vocabulary. English, for example, contains at least 615,000 words, not including technical and scientific terms. That's a tremendous vocabulary. Of those thousands of words, everyone has a slightly different meaning for each one, and things can get a little confusing. Perhaps you have experienced saying something to someone and finding that they have interpreted it completely differently from what you intended.

Ludwig Wittgenstein once said, "All the problems of philosophy are problems of language." My good friend Alex Docker adds to this, "All the problems of communication are problems of language."

Rapport is the linchpin to successful interpersonal communication. All three components of communication—physiology, tonality, and words—are essential to ensure you develop rapport with an individual or group. Rapport enables you to influence people in ways that are positive for them and to create outcomes that are win-wins. At any time in the communication process, if there is a sign of resistance, it may be due to lack of rapport. Developing rapport is a very important skill to learn, because with rapport we can alleviate any resistance to what is being communicated.

Like Attracts Like

The other principle of rapport, as I mentioned earlier, is based on the idea that like attracts like. People who are similar tend to like each other. There is a certain level of comfort in being with people who are similar to you. Haven't you ever had a time when you met someone and you felt as if you had known him or her before? This feeling of connection can also be felt when you meet someone who has experienced something that you have. A level of mutual understanding and empathy occurs that instantaneously elevates the conversation to a more familiar and open level.

This feeling of familiarity is often a result of the commonalities you share either at the conscious or unconscious level. Rapport can also be thought of as being a state of trust and responsiveness.

Interestingly enough, however, individuals can be in rapport without necessarily liking or even agreeing with each other. How is that possible? Simply by communicating in a way that is understood by the other person. In such a case, creating unconscious connection is an essential part of that comprehension equation. This is an important distinction.

Sometimes it is necessary to communicate with someone in a way that most people would consider dangerous to rapport in order to actually create it. Until his death in 1980, psychiatrist Dr. Milton Erickson was considered a master of rapport and the world's foremost authority on hypnosis. Dr. Erickson would occasionally come close to what some would call "insulting" his patients and still maintain magnificent rapport.

One particular story about Dr. Erickson illustrates this well. A client came to see him because she was overweight. She said she was ashamed because she never had time to spend with her children because she was always too busy. According to the client, she was too busy eating and buying candy and cookies. Dr. Erickson leaned over to the client and said, "You *should* be ashamed. I feel sorry for your poor children, growing up in Phoenix, Arizona, and never having had the opportunity to visit the Botanical Gardens, or to climb Squaw Peak, or see the Grand Canyon . . ." He proceeded to list several other local outdoor sites, then said, "Now go and hang a sign on your bathroom mirror that says '*Let the damn kids grow up in ignorance,*' and you need not look in the mirror, but every time you do, you will be reminded of your kids who will be disenfranchised and grow up not having had the opportunity to see and experience this wonderful place." A year later the woman contacted Dr. Erickson and said, "The kids and I have visited all the sites in and around Phoenix and I've lost twenty pounds. Can I please take that sign off the mirror?!"

If Dr. Erickson had attempted to be nicer in his interaction with the woman or to be liked by her, he might not have achieved the responsiveness that he did by communicating in such a direct manner, which got the desired result. His desired outcome was to help this lady and her desired outcome was to lose weight. Both goals were achieved because he was able to communicate effectively through establishing the correct rapport up front.

Matching and Mirroring Physiology

The process for creating a deep, unconscious rapport is to match and mirror the person with whom you are communicating. This might sound a bit strange, but the only thing strange about it is that you are bringing into conscious awareness what you have already done unconsciously with those whom you do have rapport.

If you ever stop and watch people who are engaged in deep conversation and very responsive to one another, you may notice that they are unconsciously matching and mirroring each other. You might find that they match and mirror body posture, head tilt, gestures, volume in speech, or the tempo of their speech. They may be sitting the same way, and if one is leaning forward the other is also leaning forward.

This same type of deep rapport can be created with volition at any time we choose, within a matter of seconds, simply by matching and mirroring the person we are communicating with. Now I have had people take me to task on this and say, "Well, Chris, that seems contrived and manipulative." I assure you these skills are about honoring someone's communication style and caring enough to communicate in a way that is most acceptable and comfortable to him or her. The wonderful thing about rapport is that when someone else is in rapport with you, then you are also in rapport with him or her. Rapport really offers the potential for making communication a win-win. It's the first step to successful negotiating, which I discuss in more detail in Chapter 15.

For example, have you ever had the experience of talking to someone who didn't respond in any way, and it felt as if the two of you were very disconnected? Or someone who talked so fast you couldn't get a word in edgewise? It's uncomfortable to be out of rapport with someone. If we can learn skills to consciously stop this from happening, then it's a win-win all round.

The process for instantaneous rapport was discovered when researchers Richard Bandler and John Grinder were modeling Dr. Milton Erickson and observing how he was able to create such successful connections with his clients. They noticed that he would constantly sit like his clients did, and when they moved he would seem to move as well. Erickson was a master of rapport and he placed much emphasis on its use. He was once quoted as saying, "Anything is possible in the presence of a good rapport."

I remember one of the times that I experienced the powerful effects of using rapport. A few years back, I was just starting a business partnership with an acquaintance of mine whom I hadn't seen in years. Interestingly enough, both of us had received extensive training in the techniques of establishing the deep, unconscious rapport that I am describing. When I first sat down to speak with him about our new business venture, I immediately became aware of the fact that we were matching and mirroring each other. Of course, if I hadn't been trained in the technique, I wouldn't have noticed this. At first I asked myself whether he was mirroring me consciously, or whether I was unconsciously mirroring him? It felt so comfortable, and we were getting along so tremendously, it was as if we were the closest of friends. Soon my conscious awareness of it disappeared completely. The truth was, matching and mirroring as a tool for improved communication had become so second nature to both of us that we did it automatically, without even attempting to do it consciously.

One of my favorite stories of the use of rapport came from one of my clients whom I trained to use rapport to increase his power and influence. He was a politician running for the U.S. Senate, and he was used to people recognizing him everywhere and approaching him in a friendly manner. One day he was out getting contributions for his campaign, and he stopped by the office of the president of the local Teamsters Union. My politician friend walked into the office accompanied by his campaign manager. The president of the union was on the telephone and he motioned indignantly for them to sit down. After a while the president hung up the phone, looked at my friend's campaign manager, and said in a harsh tone, "Who are you?" The teamster president knew who my friend and his manager were, but he was obviously playing hardball. My friend introduced both himself and his campaign manager. He knew that he was going to have to turn the situation around, as they certainly weren't being warmly welcomed. The teamster said, "You tell me why I should even consider contributing *anything* to your campaign." My friend stood up and walked across the room toward the union leader. He placed his hand on the shoulder of this man and began immediately to match and mirror him. He matched his breathing and his tonality, the phrases he used, and his keywords. He later told me that as soon as he started to do this, the man practically "melted." Not only did he contribute to the campaign but he became a major supporter.

The secret to making the rapport techniques work is to do it just outside of the conscious awareness of the person you are communicating with. This means if you are matching and mirroring gestures the person uses, you wouldn't do them simultaneously with the individual. You wait until it's your turn to speak and then you make similar gestures. This way they feel the connection between you at an unconscious level.

Representational Systems

People communicate and internally process information quite differently. By understanding how individuals process information we can match our communication to their processing style and create an even deeper rapport, once again, at the unconscious level.

We take in information via the five senses: visual, auditory, kinesthetic, olfactory, and gustatory. This can also be described as pictures, sounds, feelings, smells, and tastes. Most people will have what is called a preferred representational system. This is the system that they rely on predominately to process information. It is important to point out, however, that everyone is using all of the representational systems simultaneously (providing there is no neurological damage or trauma). They will simply have one system that is most familiar to them or most comfortable to rely on. People will usually be predominantly visual, auditory, or kinesthetic in their processing and, as a result, in their communication style, too.

There is a fourth category as well, which is known as auditory digital. Auditory digital simply means the self-talk we have going on inside our heads. Some people prefer to process things through their internal dialogue. It is easy to notice someone's preferred representational system once you know what to watch for. Let's examine some of the most obvious indicators of each representational system and how to tailor a message directly within that system.

Visual Representational System

Approximately 40 percent of the population is visual, so they will comprise a large portion of your team. People who are predominantly visual tend to speak at a fairly fast rate. These are people who process in pictures. You've heard before that "a picture paints a thousand words." So people who process visually will process faster than they can actually verbalize. This is why they speak so quickly. They tend to breathe high in the chest. They move from place to place rather quickly and may have difficulty just sitting around. Visual processors also tend to use visual predicates in their speech. Predicates are simply words that we use to describe our experiences. They may say things like, "Do you see what I mean?" or "I get the picture," or "I've got this thing mapped out clearly."

When making a purchase, visual processors will be interested in the look of something. They will need to "see what you're talking about" before investing. In making a decision, it will have to "appear to be" the right course of action. Visual people learn best by seeing things or by watching demonstrations. Slides, flipcharts, and diagrams are their best tools for learning.

In communicating your vision to individuals who are visual processors, you can also match your communication to their preference and thereby create a deeper interest on their part. Match the predicates that they use and speak in visual terms. To teach them or give them instructions, show visual people exactly how to do what it is that they are learning. Use charts, graphs, and other types of visual aids. In speeches and presentations, paint vivid pictures and description through your language to make things clear and compelling for them. Whether you are one-on-one or in front of a group, you can mirror their large gestures and check in with them from time to time by saying, "Do you see what I mean?" Or "You get the picture, right?"

Auditory Representational System

Next, are the auditory processors. Roughly 20 percent of the population has either auditory tonal or auditory digital preferences. Here is how you can get them on board. People who are primarily auditory will be most interested in how things sound to them. They will be very aware of the tonality of your voice. Often an auditory person's vocal qualities will be well modulated; they might even sound like a television presenter or a radio announcer. The language they use to describe their experience will be with words like, "That sounds good," "That rings a bell," or "You're coming through loud and clear." Let their language guide you to the most effective way to speak to them where they're at. They need to be told, not shown, how you feel and what exactly you want them to do. They often require verbal feedback.

When buying something, auditory people will be most interested in whether or not it "sounds" like a good purchase. An audio presentation will best connect them to your product. In making a decision, it will need to "sound" like the right thing to do. In learning something new, the sound effects used will be quite important in enabling them to integrate it and recall it later, or remember the exact wording you used.

The auditory preference is split in that there are people who process primarily auditorily, or auditory tonal, and auditory digital (or self-talk). In order to make distinctions between the two, I discuss auditory digital as an entirely different category.

Auditory Tonal

With the auditory tonal person we can create a deeper rapport and understanding by matching their predicates, saying things like, "How does that sound?" or "Does that resonate well with you?" We can facilitate their learning most effectively by speaking in pleasant tones and using a lot of vocal variation to hold their attention. They will be very sensitive to the tonality of voice and key words used by those they communicate with.

Auditory Digital

People who are auditory digital tend to process things primarily through the secondary experience of internal dialogue, "digital" simply referring to the individual words they use internally. They have a high need to talk to themselves about their subjective experience and make sense of it all, because to them it is the "logical thing to do." They will repeat things back to themselves to consider what you've said. People who are primarily auditory digital processors will be interested in logic and reason. In making decisions, the choice must always make sense. Often, even in things such as romantic relationships, they have reasonable criteria for their decisions and prefer to be told that they're loved. They will choose to be with someone because it makes sense. The pros will outweigh the cons.

In making purchases, auditory digital processors will most likely be interested in analyzing or going over all of the features of what they are considering purchasing, to make sure that it meets all of their criteria for making a logical decision. When teaching or speaking to people who process highly in the auditory digital representational system, it is important to give them lots of facts and figures, as they are interested in research and data to prove things that have been said are true.

Auditory digital people may sometimes seem slightly dissociated or removed when you are communicating with them. You can create deeper levels of rapport with the auditory digital processors by mirroring any dissociation. You can assist them in making a decision by showing logical reasons for action. You can also increase their understanding of a certain subject or topic by matching this processing style.

Kinesthetic Representational System

Roughly 40 percent of the population are primarily kinesthetic processors. People who are primarily kinesthetic processors will tend to speak very slowly and deliberately. They may go inside and check their feelings about what they are going to say before verbalizing it. Kinesthetic processors will talk about their feelings, and the predicates they use will involve touch and feeling. They will say things like, "I don't feel right about that," "I really need to get a grasp on that concept," or "I want to get in touch with her."

When making a purchase, kinesthetic processors need to "feel good about it." They certainly need to try clothes on before they buy them, to make sure they "feel right." In teaching kinesthetic processors, it's important to include exercises so that they can actually do what is being taught and get "a feel for it." People who are kinesthetic will often make decisions based on their gut instinct.

You can create deeper rapport with people who are kinesthetic by matching their breathing, which is generally low in the belly; by slowing down; by using kinesthetic predicates to describe experience; and by avoiding large, exaggerated gestures or lists of reasons.

Matching and Mirroring Voice

There are several components of the voice that we can mirror. The primary components are the tone, tempo, timbre, and volume. However, the easiest way to match and mirror voice is to stick to tempo and volume. It is quite easy to match the speed at which someone is speaking, as well as the volume, without appearing to be mimicking them.

Remember that matching works best outside of conscious awareness, so it needs to be subtle. Mirroring a voice can be particularly powerful on the telephone.

Key Words

Other things that can be matched include key words or phrases that the person uses. Key words can be any words that you hear the person say unusually often.

These can be very useful in selling. Whether you are selling products, services, or ideas, they can assist you in the communication process. One of the most important things a salesperson can do is to *listen!* Clients *will* tell you how to best communicate your offer for maximum success. Use your sensory acuity to be aware when they are conveying their needs directly or indirectly.

Everyone has a particular way of expressing themselves. If you pay attention to the subtlety of people's language you can mirror phrases they use back to them. This has the effect of making an unconscious connection so that the other person feels comfortable and understood.

You will know when someone is in rapport with you just by how the conversation is progressing. It feels very easy and comfortable. Another great clue is pacing and leading. This is when you change your physiology in some way and the person you are communicating with unconsciously follows you. For example, you might be sitting with your legs crossed, and as you uncross them the person you are communicating with will uncross his or her legs simultaneously or within a few moments thereafter.

Breaking Rapport

Sometimes it is highly appropriate to break rapport. There are some people who you may choose not to be in rapport with. There are some people in the world who do not have your highest intention in mind, and it may not be appropriate to ever enter into rapport with them. Also, if someone is not respecting your personal boundaries, either knowingly or unknowingly, it may be necessary to break rapport. The process is easy to do. It's as simple as breaking eye contact and turning away. A good and effective way to break rapport is to do it with no negativity toward the other person. Simply move away from them. This will allow you to preserve your boundaries, while not antagonizing them.

Always remember that rapport opens the gateway to communication. It's a powerful way of opening up dialogue so that you can then create synergistic relationships. Rapport-building techniques are not a means to an end. They are the beginning of a process that is developed and nurtured through trust and helping others get what they want. Ultimately, this leads to getting what you want.

14

Values—The Key to Influence and Inspiration

I consider my ability to arouse enthusiasm
among men the greatest asset I possess.
—Charles Schwab

Master communicators throughout history all seem to have an innate gift of knowing what others need and want, and finding a way of delivering that within the bigger context of what they themselves also want. The ability to mobilize, motivate, and inspire others is a skill that some believe leaders are just born with. I disagree. Anyone can develop leadership skills if they pay attention to people's needs and understand their values.

Remember, values are simply what is important to people. We have talked about them earlier in the context of clarifying your own values and how they have an impact on your reality. Here we will be looking at how to recognize and understand other people's values. By doing so you can enlist people into your vision and gain leverage in a way that ensures they get what they want while moving your vision forward, too. Because everyone has a different model of the world, it is valuable to be able to recognize key indicators of that model, and therefore what motivates someone. You then have the opportunity to explain your vision, a proposal, or a sale in the language that the other person relates to. This increases the chances of synergy and involvement considerably.

Evolution of Values

The model of values that follows comes from Dr. Clare Graves, formerly a professor at Union University in Tennessee. What's interesting about this work is that, rather than being based on hypothesis, it is the result of detailed research on people and history.

According to Graves, individuals, societies, and cultures go through an evolution of values systems, or ways of thinking about and perceiving their world that tend toward certain behavior patterns. They then cycle through each progressive value level as a reaction to the inadequacies of the previous level. Each value level is a response to the previous one in an upward spiral. It has been said that the solutions of today are the problems of tomorrow, and that's how it is with this values spiral. Each value level has its own inherent issues. Therefore, each new level upwards must adapt the thinking of the previous level to address the new wave of issues that arise.

An understanding and awareness of these different levels of thought from which people operate will increase a thousandfold your communication mastery and, therefore, your ability to produce results with and through your team. Thoroughly learning this information alone will make you an extraordinary communicator because of the meta perspective it provides of people's different, yet coexisting, models of the world. I will give you an overview of values levels first as evolving global thought systems, and then discuss in more depth how they are manifested on an individual basis and how you can apply this information to improve your daily communication. The eight values levels are described by Dr. Clare Graves in the following paragraphs in terms of both societal and human behavior.

Values Level 1—Survival

This level doesn't really exist in society today, other than in newborn babies, but it was prevalent in early times before people banded together in tribes. It is very instinctive and represents our physical nature, the basic drive to survive. A newborn child, for example, is only interested in eating and sleeping and doing what it needs to do to survive. As humans developed, however, they realized it was just too hard to survive on their own, so they started to band together to form tribes. Thus, over time, they evolved to values level 2.

Values Level 2—Tribal

This values level was reached when people started to come together to form tribes because it was the best form of protection. This level included subservience and an expectation of sacrifice for the chief. As evolution has taken place, however, ego has emerged more strongly and the drive for power has overridden the sacrifice mentality as new potential chiefs vie for power.

Values Level 3—Aggression and Power

This is the values level of "might is right," where the strong dominate the weak, and rebellion is the order of the day. What happens in this level is that the young challenge the old. Over time there is a realization that this cannot continue, so a desire for systems and stability emerges.

Values Level 4—Systems

This is the value level that says there is one best way, that system and order are good. Obedience and discipline take over from the previous level of risk, aggression, and disorder. Here we earn reward by hard work and order. Authority is king, and we seek to belong to a system and find comfort from being part of the collective. This is the home of rigid thinking; many of the "isms" emerge at this level of thinking—communism, Catholicism, terrorism, and so forth. Most of the world religions fall into values level 4 thinking, which can be stated as "Sacrifice now for reward later."

As evolution progresses, the urge to break free from that rigidity by rebelling shows up once again. There is a move to break out and seek reward, which brings about the next level.

Values Level 5—Success

This is the level most concerned with achievement. The mottos of the success oriented might be, "Make it happen!" and "Just do it!" It's the level where the world is a marketplace for entrepreneurs to profit. The level is often materialistic, although the motivation is often more about the sense of achievement that comes from the accumulation of material wealth rather than the material wealth itself. The evolution of this level is that people get to a later stage in life and realize that all that accumulation hasn't made them happy or complete, and they feel a hole in their soul. This is often when they move on to the next level.

Values Level 6—Group and Cause Oriented

This is where people turn inward instead of outward for fulfillment and happiness. Happiness is not dependent on the number of toys or material possessions but rather on a sense of contribution and community. The drawback of level 6 thinking is that it can become too democratic. When everyone is equal and has a right to their opinion as truth, sometimes in the quest for consensus nothing actually gets done. This can also be the most controlling values level because it may preach love and acceptance of everybody, but you are loved and accepted only if you also love and accept everybody. This causes frustration again due to the lack of tangible results. The bonding may feel good but there is inevitably a move to make things happen more effectively, and people move to the next level.

Values Level 7—Functional Flow

The drive for individuality pushes through and breaks out of the mold of seeking acceptance. There is an understanding of the paradoxical nature of the world. To experience life you must experience *all* of life, not just the pockets of acceptable behavior. People who function on this level will not turn their backs on the causes and ideals of level 6, but will instead be focused on living those ideals, while also breaking away from the group and exploring all that life has to offer. Level 7 people are constantly learning. They will listen and take in a great deal of differing views. They will take on what they choose and what feels right for them at that time, but they are not set in their views. They are flexible in their thinking and are not overly attached to anything, be it ideas, beliefs, or physical possessions. Values level 7 is the first values level that is able to move throughout all the previous levels with volition, depending upon what works best at the time.

The downside to level 7 is that sooner or later the exploring lone wolf gets bored and perhaps lonely, and then, lacking any concrete goals, once again begins moving on to the next level, searching for something more meaningful.

Values Level 8—The Planet Does Matter

Values level 8 people begin to look at the world in a new way. They see the world as being one living entity and themselves being a microcosm of the macrocosm. They are most interested in who they become as a result of how they relate to the whole.

The reason these values levels are important to you as you hone your leadership skills is that truly understanding them allows you to tailor your communication to every individual on your team, at the values level suitable to the individual, so that your vision relates to each one in the way most compelling to him or her. The results are, first, an even greater level of rapport, and secondly, you have linked your communication to those values that truly motivate and inspire them.

For example, when you can determine that someone's thinking resides mostly in values level 5, you can construct your proposal to that person very differently than you would a proposal to a level 6 person, emphasizing those things that fulfill the individual's uniquely level 5 motivations. Say, for example, you have written a book and you are sitting down to propose it to a publisher. If that publisher has mentioned how hard he worked to get where he is and that he is looking to become senior editor, because the prestige and notoriety are important to him, his thinking is likely centered at values level 5, perhaps even with some level 4, demonstrated by his loyalty to the company. After listening to his communication about what is important to him, you may decide to say, "My last book sold 500,000 copies worldwide, which generated $6 million. This new one I just wrote is likely to do the same if not better."

If your publisher had spent more of your conversation talking about how much she loves her job because of all the people the company helps with their books and because of the impact she is making on the conscious-minded community, she would be demonstrating more level 6 thinking. Then your previous pitch wouldn't be nearly as effective, and would likely fall flat, because money and status may not be as high on her list of values. She may even abreact to those level 5 values, judging them as selfish, and therefore reject your book without consciously realizing why! Instead you could say, "I have written a new book. As you know, I am dedicated to the expansion of human consciousness and providing information and tools so that everyone can find their place in the world and find happiness and fulfillment." Sure, you would also add the dollars, but it is not the dollars that will inspire a level 6 person. Remember that you should only say things if they are actually true, but if you are communicating with someone of a specific values level, you can simply tailor your communication to fit their model of the world.

When you are aware of someone's values level, you can speak their language to get them inspired and involved in your vision while also letting them feel as though they are furthering their own cause and what is important to them. This is a perfect win-win. (As long as what you say is also true. Remember to keep your communication ecological in that your objectives are safe for everyone.)

Recognizing Values through Behavior

Remember that these aren't types of people but rather systems of thought inside people. These categories aren't intended to pigeonhole people but, rather, to serve as useful information when communicating with them. Also remember that someone may be a combination of different levels in different areas of life. Someone may demonstrate, for example, level 5 thinking in business and level 3 in relationships.

To assist you in recognizing the different levels, here are some more things to watch out for when figuring out what is important to the people with whom you're dealing.

The odd-numbered values levels, 1, 3, 5, and 7, are focused on self, whereas the even-numbered value levels, 2, 4, 6, and 8, are focused on others and sacrificing for others. The odd and even values levels also see their locus of control as coming from different areas. People with an odd-numbered values level see their locus of control as being internal. In other words, they perceive themselves as being in control of their own destiny. The even-numbered values levels believe that the locus of control is external. It's about the external world and how they relate to it as part of a community.

Interestingly enough, however, the focus is different also. While the odd numbers think of themselves as being in control, their focus is on creating the external world the way they want it. So they use that internal power to design the external world around them. With the sacrificial levels 2, 4, 6, and 8, the locus of control is external yet their focus is internal. They are interested in working out who they become as a result of what they are doing with the group or the cause—how they feel about themselves as a result of doing what they do.

Recognizing What Motivates People

Values levels play a large role in determining how people are motivated. Values level 1 people exist as part of nature, acting instinctively, much like other animals. Values level 2 people show tribal tendencies, banding together for safety to placate spirits and nature. Their ritualistic behaviors are motivated by their sense that the external world is full of mystery and danger beyond their ability to control.

Values level 3 people think "it's a jungle out there." Their behavior shows their belief in the survival of the fittest, where each must fend for him- or herself, control or be controlled.

Values level 4 individuals are strongly influenced by a need for structure and the belief that the world is controlled by a higher power, whether that represents a divine entity, the church, or the company where they've worked for 50 years. They are motivated by doing the right thing; therefore, they tend to be driven by a sense of guilt. If they are not doing the right thing, they believe they should feel guilty or be punished accordingly. This belief would obviously have a strong governing influence over a person's behavior. As a result, these people will obey, often without question, whomever they believe to be the rightful authority.

Values level 5 individuals see the world as being full of opportunities for materialistic gain. Therefore, they can tend to be opportunistic or go-getters, relating everything to money and how it could serve them on their drive to succeed. Level 5 behaviors might be motivated by that old 1980s motto, "He who dies with the most toys wins." They also like to be in control because they know best what's right for them personally. Therefore, they operate best with autonomy and authority, such as running their own businesses.

Value level 6 people live life with wider social concerns, feeling they are part of a larger, connected humanity. Personal growth and a shared sense of community are important to them. They feel good when they are contributing to society.

Values level 7 people perceive the world around them as a complex system at risk of collapse. They are primarily motivated by learning, being free, and questioning the way things are. They change and explore the world as it serves their interests at the time.

Values level 8 people seek balance and order beneath the Earth's chaos. These seemingly rare individuals maintain a global perspective in all of their actions because they are aware of the interdependence of all living things. They are motivated by whatever benefits the whole system.

Recognizing Values through Decision-Making Criteria

The following are the criteria that each level would typically use when making decisions. What types of activities people choose to be involved in or which proposals to accept, even what cars to buy, are determined by what is important to them—their primary values. These responses show what each level would consider when deciding whether something is a good idea or the right thing for them to do. As you read this, be thinking about how you can apply all this information to better understand your own values and choices as well as who to choose to assist you in reaching your goals.

We needn't go into level 1 people here because they no longer exist from a cultural perspective, and as babies would not be engaging in any decision-making processes.

Level 2: Because the "tribe" or social group is central to their existence, level 2 people will decide to do something based on whether their leader or boss approves. They are generally followers who want to be told what to do.

Level 3: Because immediate rewards are paramount to level 3 people and they tend to act impulsively, they will choose what's best to do by saying, "Let's do it! It will get me what I want right now!" They might also decide between options based on outsmarting someone else or beating them to the punch, as they see this as a dog-eat-dog world. By the way, you can't get a level 3 to rise to action using guilt, as you could a level 4—level 3 thinkers just don't feel guilt, although they can feel shame.

Level 4: Since level 4s like to follow the rules to avoid punishment and carry out their duty, they make a decision by saying, "That's the right thing to do because it's in line with the establishment." They will choose a course of action that is in line with company policy, fulfills what is expected of them by their family, or follows the law to the letter. Remember that they will be looking to comply with their group's outside authority.

Level 5: They will be looking to determine which option furthers their own ambitions or material gain. If it assists them on their way they will bend the rules and their values in any situation in order to win. This is called situational ethics. Level 5 people choose what is best for achieving their objectives, saying, "I'm going to go for it because it is to my own greater advantage."

Level 6: Having a bigger picture in mind that includes everyone, level 6 individuals will try to make decisions by consensus. They choose what to do by saying, "That's a good idea because everyone agrees."

Level 7: Level 7 people will tend to make decisions based upon how they know and feel within themselves, regardless of what others think. They take responsibility for their actions and make sure what they do is ecological, while still being egocentric. A level 7 will choose what to do by saying, "That will work best because it functions well personally and on every level."

Level 8: These people believe that collective individualism serves the entire living system, so they would take the planet into consideration when making any decisions. They seek ways to benefit the living system they are an integral part of. Level 8s will choose what to do by saying, "That's the right thing to do because it fits with nature's patterns and will benefit the whole."

Values in Self-Perception and Relationships

It's important not to judge the values levels. One is not better than the other. It's not a competition to get to the top. Some people will move through the values levels during the course of their lives and others will not. The important thing is to recognize the levels in people around you through the language they use and the behaviors and decision-making criteria they employ. You can also pick up on an individual's values level by his or her apparent self-perception and relationships to others.

Sometimes values level 6 people would like to think of themselves as 8s. The 5s want to be the best, so whatever that is, they want to be it! A 3 will look at everyone else as suckers. The 4 will see everyone as wrong and will often assume a 7 or a 5 is actually a 3. The 5 will look at an 8 as a 6 and sometimes at a 7 and see a 3.

There are also some insidious relationships that develop between the levels. For example, a 6 and a 3 may be in relationship because the 6 wants to save the 3. The 3 will like that self-serving relationship because they will think they can use the 6. The 5 will often get into a relationship with a 2 because the 2 will stay home and mind the family while the 5 goes out and creates. The 7 will stay in a relationship as long as it serves them and then move on to the next, not in a callous way but often because they've learned what they can from that relationship and are ready to explore a new dynamic.

By truly understanding the values levels, you will master a whole new skill in communication. You will be able to make your communication most compelling regardless of its content. This information is especially powerful if you can combine the values level with the more specific personal values of the individual. This can be done through either direct or indirect elicitation.

Eliciting Values

Eliciting values is a technique to use conversationally to better understand who you are doing business with, selling to, hiring, or any other relationship where you want to serve everyone's interests. If you are going to do a direct elicitation, it may be necessary to tell your client, prospect, or team member what you are about to do. This is also known as a pre-frame. When I am doing formal values elicitation with a client, I will sometimes say, "To save you time and best serve you, would it be okay if I asked you a few questions?"

Then simply ask the question, "What's important to you in a business relationship?" When you are coming from integrity, your understanding of the client's values will really assist you in creating a long-term working relationship.

You can also do formal values elicitations around the product or service someone is buying. A good example of this is a realtor representing a buyer who's looking for a new house. The question is, "What's important to you in a house?" Outstanding realtors know exactly what their buyers want.

This is also a great process when going for interviews or pitching for new business. I remember asking a prospective boss, "What's important to you in someone who works for you?" As soon as I asked that question, many things were revealed to me. He gave me a list of the following valued qualities he was seeking:

- Team player
- Learning and growing
- Enthusiastic
- Hardworking

It's a deceptively simple and seemingly obvious question to ask. Yet, you'd be surprised how many people doing business employ guesswork instead! The values elicitation provided extremely important information for me. Once I knew exactly what he wanted in an employee, I could then give examples of my past experience that demonstrated those values. Needless to say, I got the job, and it also gave me incredible peace of mind while I was working there. I never had to worry or wonder about what he thought of my work. I knew exactly what values level to satisfy. He was thrilled with my job performance and I was content and at ease knowing that I was doing the right things. I effectively sold myself to the company on a daily basis through the fulfillment of my employer's values.

Now you can use your new knowledge of values systems to inspire and motivate individuals on your team, understand what criteria people use to make decisions and recognize the best way to communicate within anyone's model of the world.

15

CHAPTER

Win-Win Sales and Negotiation

*It is one of the most beautiful compensations
of this life that no man can sincerely try to
help another without helping himself.*

—**Ralph Waldo Emerson**

In his book *40 Day Mind Fast Soul Feast,* Dr. Reverend Michael Beckwith tells us that in order to live the life we are meant to live we must "Stop working, start serving!" What he means is that the moment we come from an intention of serving others, we make our own lives more fulfilling and create the opportunity to increase our own personal prosperity. He goes on to explain, "Ralph Waldo Emerson said that we place the Universe in our debt as we give more than we are compensated for, if we don't work for mere money alone. Since we cannot out-give the self-givingness of the spirit, the Universe will create opportunities to give even more back to us than we could ever give to it."

A lot of people go through life looking for what they can get out of it. This is the least effective way of approaching things. If you are unsatisfied, it is nothing but a reflection of the value, or worth, you are adding. Instead of asking, "What can I get?" ask, "What can I give?" I guarantee you your fortune will change—almost overnight.

167

This intention is the common mark of a business that will really go somewhere and have longevity.

When you go into a situation to see what you can give and you create value for others, you are compensated for it with money, which is our means of measuring and exchanging value. If you create tremendous value for others and you do it intelligently, you will get tremendous financial rewards. This is the basis of the law of reciprocity.

Dr. Genie Laborde, in the book *Influencing With Integrity*, speaks of the process of dovetailing outcomes. This means making certain that every communication outcome you have is win-win, where both parties profit. This, I believe, is one of the most important aspects of most interpersonal interactions. When your outcomes are not win-win, you will earn a reputation as being someone who is self-serving. You may fool some people for a while, but your long-term success will be adversely affected. When your outcomes are win-win and "dovetailed," you foster good will amongst the people you deal with. You, as well as those you are involved with, will prosper, and you will earn a reputation that brings you much success. With this in mind, let's more closely examine the magic behind successful selling and negotiating.

A few years ago I was speaking at a business camp with Brian Tracy, who is known as one of America's leading sales authorities. One evening as I was having dinner with Brian, I asked him what advice he would give to someone who was just starting in business, and he said, "Never forget to sell yourself. Nobody else will do it for you. You've always got to be selling yourself."

- What makes winning politicians? Their ability to sell themselves to their constituents.
- What makes winning trial attorneys? Their ability to sell their client's case and effectively win over the judge and jury.
- What makes effective communicators of any type? Their ability to sell their ideas and concepts to others.
- What makes effective parents? Their ability to sell their values and behavioral boundaries better than those who might influence their child negatively.

Gandhi was a very intelligent lawyer skilled in persuasive communication before turning to champion the freedom of his people. He knew how to sell his ideas. This allowed him to be amazingly effective at negotiating with the British, who were in power at the time. He was equally effective in his ability to sell his ideas of nonviolence to the world. So sales and negotiating are not too different a process—selling often contains some negotiating, and successful negotiations always require a little selling. It's all about finding out what both sides need, and then filling those needs. In this chapter, you will learn the specific techniques for win-win selling and negotiating.

The Win-Win Selling Process

We are all salesmen every day of our lives. We are selling our ideas, our plans, our enthusiasms to those with whom we come in contact.

—Charles Schwab

One of the greatest gifts we have as human beings is imagination. Selling is all about leading the imagination of others to a place where they can really connect with and become inspired by the prospect of having your product, service, idea, or long-term vision. Great visionaries and leaders in history often seem to innately possess this ability, but it can also be broken down into steps and learnable skills.

Learning to powerfully sell your ideas is essential to your success in any field. The following is a precise, easy to remember selling process that will allow you to lead people's minds and hearts in a way that compels them to take the actions you suggest. To make it easier to recall the steps in any situation, just think of the following acronym:

S.O.A.R. to R.I.C.H.E.S.

S.O.A.R. represents all the information you need to elicit from your prospect in order to sell your product or idea. It is usually obtained during the interview phase of the process. By interviewing I mean getting to understand the prospect better; this can occur throughout the course of a client/prospect relationship, whether you have two years or two minutes with this person. Here is what it stands for:

S. Situation: Find out about the client's current situation.

O. Objectives: Find out what the client wants right now.

A. Antecedent: Find out what stands in the client's way of having what he or she wants—whatever must be overcome before getting his or her rewards.

R. Rewards: Find out what rewards the client will ultimately obtain by reaching his or her objectives.

R.I.C.H.E.S. represents all the things that need to take place in order for there to be a buying commitment:

R. Rapport.

I. Interview.

C. Course of action.

H. How would you like to pay for that?

E. Excite the client.

S. Serve and satisfy.

Remember that we are always selling something. So when I use the terms *prospect* or *client*, keep in mind how this process serves *your* unique situation. A prospect could be an individual you are considering hiring for your team, a company you are making a proposal to, or even someone you want to invite away with you for the weekend (in which case the step "How would you like to pay for that?" would probably not apply!). In any case, utilize all you can. It works. I know from experience. It is one of the fastest and most effective ways to get to a win-win buying commitment.

First, S.O.A.R. covers the specific information you need to obtain during the interview process. It represents the "I" in R.I.C.H.E.S., which I will cover later.

Interview Questioning Flow

Asking questions is one of the most important aspects of win-win selling because you discover what is most important to your prospect, which tells you what will compel them toward taking action. Once you've established rapport, the interview phase gets you to better understand the client's needs and values. That's why it is sometimes termed *gap analysis*—discovering where the client is now, where he or she wants to be, and whether your product, service, or idea can bridge the gap.

My good friend Joe Hasson of Thomas Kiblen and Associates calls this questioning stage the "heart of the sale." He uses the analogy of an artichoke. What is the best part of an artichoke? The heart is. To get to the heart you've got to peel away the leaves and scoop out the gunk on top. That's the questioning process. S.O.A.R questioning is extremely effective. Here's how you do it:

S. Situational Questions

Situational questions allow us to understand the current situation of a prospect, prospective client, or employer. They tell us about the company or the individual. This also assists us in deepening rapport and building credibility because it shows that we are genuinely interested in this person or group.

Think for a moment about what it is you are selling. Are you selling your products or services? Are you selling yourself for a promotion or a raise? What is it that you sell? If your answer is "nothing," think again. If you *were* selling something, what would it be?

In selling sales trainings, for example, we would ask the following types of situational questions:

- How many people do you have in your company?
- How long have you been working here?
- How did you choose to get into this line of work?
- How many sales are you making on a monthly basis?

Situational questions draw out a person's current situation. It's a good idea to write your own list of situation questions and memorize them so that you don't have to try to come up with questions during the interview. You can instead fully focus on and stay present with your prospect, creating a deeper rapport.

Write down six situation questions that you could ask someone with whom you may find yourself in a selling situation in the near future:

1. _____
2. _____
3. _____
4. _____
5. _____
6. _____

O. Objective Questions

Objective questions allow us to better understand what the other party wants to achieve in life or in business. The presupposition inherent in asking the questions, "What should you be doing?" or "What do you want to be doing instead?" is that the person is not currently doing it. This will tell you what the client or prospect would like to have happen instead, the ultimate goals and objectives that you will be able to assist him or her to achieve.

Again, using the scenario of selling a sales training or going into a company as a business consultant, here are some sample questions you can ask to reveal a person's objectives:

- What should you be doing?
- How much business is your top salesperson doing?
- How do you rate in comparison with your competition?
- What are your current goals?
- How close are you to your current goals?
- What expectations do you have of yourself or your department?

Once again, take a few moments now to write down six objective questions to ask the same person you were thinking about in the previous exercise:

1. _____

2. _____

3. _____

4. _____

5. _____

6. _____

A. Antecedent Questions

It's time to ask the antecedent questions, what comes *before* the reward. These questions give the consultative salesperson important information about what they believe is opposing their efforts, what is preventing the client, prospect, or individual from accomplishing their goals. Much in the same way that a therapist probes for what is causing problems, a consultative salesperson looks for the perceived barriers to success. Examples of questions that reveal this type of information are as follows:

- What is preventing you from having what you want in your business or life?
- What has stopped you from creating the type of results that you want?
- What's stopped you from training your other salespeople to produce as much as your top salesperson?
- What is getting in your way?

Take a moment now to write six antecedent type questions:

1. _____

2. _____

3. _____

4. _____

5. _____

6. _____

R. Reward Questions

Finally, we are left with reward questions. These questions essentially supply us with the individual's positive "toward" motivation for taking action and influencing behavior. What specific benefits will the person get by eliminating the barriers and producing the stated objectives? What will the end result be? And what will they potentially miss out on if they don't take action? An easy question to ask is:

- When you have (the stated goal), what will that get for you or allow you to do?

This question will reveal to you the ultimate reward for the individual with whom you're working. You are now tapping into their dream or vision. The prize for having reached their objectives could be anything from world recognition to a world cruise.

Quite often, a person's first response to a reward question will not provide enough information for the effective consultative salesperson to see how he or she can assist them to fulfill that dream. It's necessary to find out more. The way to do this is to tap into the person's values. Ask:

- What's important to you about that?

When the person gives you the initial reward answer, you say,

- What's important to you about that?

Then ask:

- When you have (the reward), what will you be doing?

This will provide valuable information to be used later in the selling process. The idea behind these final questions is to ascertain the individual's values around the situation and, specifically, how the solution could tap into those values.

Take a moment now to write six reward type questions for your prospect:

1. _____

2. _____

3. _____

4. _____

5. _____

6. _____

When you know how to engage the imagination of your prospect using the S.O.A.R questioning technique, you have all you need to truly engage your prospect.

Steps to R.I.C.H.E.S.

I wanted to first fill you in on what your interview questions will be. However, you will actually begin to soar to riches by establishing rapport.

R. Rapport

The first step in the win-win selling process is to develop rapport. However, rapport should be maintained throughout your whole encounter because the essence of rapport is having that person stay responsive to you. There are countless ways to do that. People stay connected with you when they know you sincerely care about their needs. You're not just making a sale; you are making a friend. So ask yourself how you would act with a friend. You talk about your mutual interests, inquire about the friend's needs and desires, share stories. . . . You might even give a friend a gift. And one of the best gifts you can give to someone, one that means the most, is to listen. Don't underestimate how great you make someone feel by just listening. Consider what makes you feel connected to someone else, and then offer the same. Know that people will sense if you are not sincere. Creating rapport doesn't mean doing whatever it takes to get them to like or agree with you, including false claims. In fact, rapport happens when your words and actions ring true, so keep it real. And practice those rapport skills you learned in Chapter 13. Whenever a conversation seems stuck or you've just about given up on it, it is amazing how rapport alone can turn around any outcome to one you intended.

I. Interview

Asking questions is the only way to sell. This is where the S.O.A.R. criteria for interviewing come in to play and where the art of really listening is so vital. The effective salesperson is not the person who talks people into things they don't need or want. An effective salesperson is a matchmaker between a product, service, or idea and the people that need or want it. To presume that you know what everyone needs without knowing anything about them is to close the doors to the magic that makes true sales professionals successful.

One of the most important aspects of modern selling is to use a consultative approach—not closing sales but, instead, opening relationships. Outstanding salespeople become highly valued consultants to the person or group they are working with. The best consultants are explorers and discoverers. They uncover where they can be of assistance and assist their prospects to make the connections that cause them to want to buy. The first step is to uncover vital information about their values and desires. Much in the same way that an archaeologist digs for hidden treasures that lie buried beneath the surface, the salesperson can excavate what clients truly want and need by questioning what their situation is, their objectives, any barriers, and the rewards they are ultimately seeking.

Test close questions are a good way then to check in with the prospect and gauge where he or she is in the sales process. As you begin to connect your product with the person's true motivations and desires, you can make sure along the way that you're both still in agreement by using questions as simple as, "Does that sound good to you so far?" If the person is answering "yes" with each test close, and showing other buying signals such as leaning forward, smiling enthusiastically, or even reaching for a wallet, you are moving inevitably forward toward your sale. Because you are addressing all the prospect's objections along the way, you will not be hit with them suddenly at the end as you are pulling out your pen. Sometimes it will be clear to you by paying attention to your prospect's buying signals that he or she is ready to move forward right away. If that's the case, cut to the chase. Show them the dotted line.

Even knowing what people *don't* want will serve you by telling you what they are motivated to move *away* from. Surprisingly, people react much more quickly to avoid pain than to move toward something they want. We all take much quicker action to pull our hand away from a hot stove than we do in reaching for the refrigerator. An amazing number of people live in denial of their real issues, in terms of what the problem is and why they aren't getting what they want in their career or their lives. We do them a great disservice if we don't get them to see what's not working and to access their discomfort or discontent about it. It is often the negative feelings that finally motivate people to take constructive action and finally move forward. This means, in order to gain true leverage, you can get people to associate or link not having your product with experiencing discomfort. If toward motivation isn't compelling enough for them to see your vision, away-from motivation can move them to respond faster. No one wants to get burned. All of this can be done through questioning during the S.O.A.R. interview process.

C. Course of Action

From the interview, you have ascertained whether they have a need or want that you can solve. If they don't, you thank them and leave. If they do, you get them to see how you can help them fulfill their objectives and rewards. Since you have taken the necessary time to listen and ascertain what is most important to them, you have done enough trial closes along the way to address any objections or concerns on their part, and you are in a position to close the deal with certainty that you can serve and satisfy them. The next step is to use the power of assumption and simply lay out the best course of action by saying, "Here's how we're going to solve your problem" or "get you what you want." Then add your description of how they can use your product, service, or idea. You are now showing them exactly how they can fulfill the desires you uncovered earlier. This basically serves as the final close because you've already answered their concerns throughout the interview. The rest is just working out the details.

H. How Would You Like to Pay for It?

If you've done your job correctly up front—gained rapport, asked questions, provided the right solutions—gaining buying commitment is as simple as asking, "How do you want to pay for it?" A lot of people put too much emphasis on closing. Closing the sale just means asking for the order. When you go to Kmart and go up to the checkout counter with your purchases, the cashier doesn't make a big deal about asking, "How do you want to pay for it?" Frankly, closing is the easiest part.

E. Excite Your Client

You always want to excite your clients not just about your product or proposal, but about the benefits of how it will serve their desires. I emphasize their wants over their needs because it is their deepest wants that truly motivate people toward action. Your own conviction and enthusiasm about your product will transfer from you to them. Transfer your own excitement to them, then have them associate, link in their mind, your product with what would give them the most pleasure.

This can be done in a couple of different ways. One is through the use of end-result imagery. You used your own end-result imagery when you set your goals in the C.R.E.A.T.E. format and visualized your end step. End-result imagery becomes equally effective when applied to the process of selling. The image represents what they want to receive, including the positive emotional state, from your product. You assist the buyer to access their imagination to create a visual image and a corresponding positive emotional state about how your product, service, or idea will enrich their life.

For example, if your prospect said that the ultimate reward from having their challenges solved is that they would be able to spend time with their family in Milan, Italy, then at the appropriate moment in the sales process you could say, "Picture this: It's six months from now, and you and your family are in Milan, enjoying yourselves, and you feel so good when you think to yourself, 'I'm sure glad I took that sales training, because that's what's allowed me to create this.' That's what you want, right?" Even a question like, "Wouldn't that be great?" gets them saying yes. Once they have agreed with you enough times, any objections they had suddenly don't weigh in as much as do their desires.

That visual fantasy can be given additional impact by working in all of the representational systems—pictures, sounds, feelings, tastes, smells, and self-talk. Exciting your client can actually be used throughout the win-win selling process wherever you deem appropriate. The full sensory experience that you create in their mind through using end-result imagery will be based on information that you have elicited in the questioning phase of the sale.

S. Serve and Satisfy the Client

The final step of the win-win selling process is not really an ending but the beginning of a long-term relationship. This step is all about serving and satisfying your client. It's been said that if you help enough people get what they want, surely you will get what you want.

A good example of this win-win selling process in action was when I was negotiating for a job with a training organization. Watch how, although I was in "negotiations," I used the win-win selling process to serve everyone well. I was negotiating back and forth with the vice president of the company, and we were hung up on the amount of money that I was to be paid if I accepted the job. At one point, through my interview, I was able to discern how much money the company pulled in, in terms of gross revenue per year (using the S.O.A.R. questioning criteria). I also asked how much they would like to be doing, and what would be a major breakthrough for them to accomplish in terms of gross revenue in the upcoming year. After I had all of this information, I said to the vice president, "Picture this: It's one year from now and your company has made 'X' millions of dollars, and you think to yourself, 'I'm sure glad I hired Chris, because he's what made this happen for us.' Is that what you'd like to see happen?" He said, "Yes!" Understanding what was important to the company I was pitching (wants and values), I was then able to get them excited about my ability to satisfy those desires. I was hired for the job. The company almost tripled their sales the following year, a result far in excess of their previous expectations. In a meeting with the entire staff, the vice president (who has since become president) credited my training as the catalyst. The arrangement had served both of us well—a win-win, as I believe all sales should be. Make certain that you can back up your promises. This is the only way to build credibility, long-term relationships, and repeat business, and ultimately attain your vision.

The Win-Win Negotiating Process

In business as in life, you don't get what
you deserve, you get what you negotiate.
—Chester L. Karrass

Negotiating is another crucial leadership skill to have during any sales process, as in most other areas of life. Whether you are negotiating with a partner to buy a property, selling one million widgets, or negotiating with your kids to take a share in the housework, the win-win negotiating process outlined in the rest of this chapter can greatly influence your level of accomplishment. It details the tools, preparation, and steps to negotiating effectively, whatever the situation, even when you do not seem to share common goals. Negotiating, as in sales, requires that you have the ability to use your language with volition, exercise flexibility and range in your thought processes, and structure your communication to lead others to a specified outcome. Possessing these specific negotiating skills that the best leaders utilize is imperative to achieving high levels of achievement.

Negotiating Tools

Let's begin with more tools for your toolbox to build success:

The Agreement Frame

The Agreement Frame is an elegant way to direct your conversation down the road you choose. It's really very simple: Never use the word *but* when attempting to persuade others or get people to see your point of view. *But* is a negation operator in language, which means that when you use it in a sentence you negate everything that comes before it. For example, if you said, "I think this is what we should do," and I said, "Yes, but we can't," even though I answered with "yes," I then contradicted that positive response with "but," which effectively made it a negative response. You may get the sense your idea has been rejected and get defensive.

If, on the other hand, I answered using "I agree, and . . ." or "I respect that, and . . ." or "I appreciate your point, and . . . ," it would have felt very different. So I could have said, "I appreciate that you are thinking of the best interests of the company, and that's exactly why I think we should do it this way . . ." It's much more elegant, gets the same outcome, and sends the conversation in the direction of agreement. That is why it's called the agreement frame. Use it and notice how much more smoothly your negotiations go.

Chunking

Chunking refers to the fact that there are many different planes of abstraction on which we can think and communicate. People chunk information differently. The first step to clarity, then, is recognizing individual styles of thinking. Language indicates the level of a person's thinking, from abstraction to specificity. At times, you will want to use this chunking skill to pace and lead others through the various levels, either up, down or laterally. You also need this skill personally to keep the larger picture, or end goal, in mind as you negotiate through the smaller details. Your ability to think on several levels of abstraction has a direct relation to your income level. Who has to think in more levels of abstraction, the CEO or the parking attendant? Who makes the larger income?

Often, the only issue obstructing communication is people speaking on different levels of abstraction and specificity. Two people could essentially be saying the same thing but one uses broader concepts while the other one uses numbers.

So when you are in negotiations with someone else, chunking can be a very useful tool in finding agreement that may not be immediately apparent. Figure 15.1 depicts the process of chunking.

Useful for:

Finding the intention behind the demand

Finding how to motivate others

Discovering new options

Negotiating

CHUNKING UP:

• Move from a specific term to the general category.

•   For agreement, alignment.

CHUNKING DOWN

• Move from the specific to the more specific or to the component parts.

•   For specificity, the "how to."

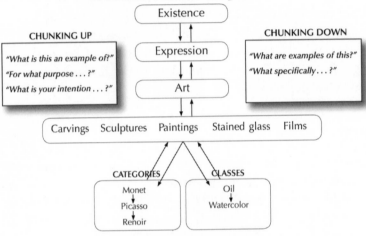

BIG PICTURE

Abstraction / Intuitor / Trance

The Structure of Overwhelm—Too Big Chunks

Existence

CHUNKING UP

"What is this an example of?"

"For what purpose . . . ?"

"What is your intention . . . ?"

Expression

CHUNKING DOWN

"What are examples of this?"

"What specifically . . . ?"

Art

Carvings   Sculptures   Paintings   Stained glass   Films

CATEGORIES

Monet
↓
Picasso
↓
Renoir

CLASSES

Oil
↓
Watercolor

CHUNKING DOWN TO DETAILS

Figure 15.1   Abstract to Specific Detail: Chunking Using the Hierarchy of Ideas

Chunking Up

Chunking up means moving from a specific term to its general category. To chunk up on an idea you can ask a number of questions:

- What is this an example of?
- What is its purpose?
- What is your intention?

If you wanted to chunk up on the idea of *car* for example, you would ask the appropriate questions from the list above. What is a car an example of? What is the purpose of a car? What is the intention of the car? One answer to these questions could be "transportation." You have just chunked up to transportation, which is a more abstract idea than car. If you then wanted to chunk up further, you would repeat the process to get to "movement," and so on. In this way, you gain flexibility and versatility, so speak on anyone's level or bring two sides to the same level.

Chunking Down

Chunking down means moving from a general category to a specific term, or from a specific term to a more specific term. To chunk down on an idea, you can ask:

- What are examples of this?
- What specifically . . . ?

To chunk down on the earlier example of *car*, you would ask, "What are examples of a car?" The answer to that could be either classes and categories of cars, such as sedans, SUVs, and coupes; or it could be parts of a car such as wheel, hubcap, and so on. Say, for example, you went to the garage and said to the mechanic, "I have a problem with my car." The mechanic is going to chunk down to get more specific information that will direct him to the cause of the problem. So the conversation may go something like this:

You: "I have a problem with my car."
Mechanic: "What specifically is wrong with your car?"
You: "I don't know, it's something to do with the wheel."
Mechanic: "What specifically is wrong with the wheel?"
You: "It's something to do with the lug nuts."
Mechanic: What specifically is wrong with the lug nuts?"
You: "They are all missing."
Mechanic: "Ah, well that's your problem."

By using this technique, one is able to identify and isolate the level of specific information necessary for problem-solving. For example, the mechanic would first clarify the make and model of the car so he could make an accurate assessment.

Lateral Chunking

You can also chunk laterally. To do this you would chunk up one level and then ask:

- What are other examples of this?

So, for the same example, if I were to chunk laterally on *car*, I would chunk up to transportation and then ask, "What are some other examples of transportation?" The answer could be buses, boats, planes, trains, and so on.

Again, this appears to be a relatively simple technique. Yet, surprisingly few businesspeople employ it. Minor negotiations can become problematic just for lack of speaking the same language or knowing where someone else is coming from. Even in everyday conversations your new awareness can prove invaluable. By practicing your ability to chunk up, down, and laterally, you will find that you start to think circles around the people you are dealing with and negotiating with. This will assist you in ways you didn't think possible in terms of arriving at win-win outcomes.

Remember that the greater your ability to think in expanded planes of abstraction, the more money you will make in the world. The ability to think through the range from specific to abstract is one of the traits of extraordinary leaders, managers, and entrepreneurs. Abstract thinking alone will not be nearly as effective as your ability to move through the entire range. Also, the person who controls the level of abstraction in a conversation controls the conversation.

From a negotiation standpoint, there is always less disagreement the more you chunk up, so the more abstract an idea, the less room there is to disagree. And if you are able to gracefully achieve a positive response by dealing in the abstract first, you then create positive momentum, which assists in the final specific agreement.

For example, say you go into a business to help the two owners negotiate a prickly, persistent issue. The first owner says, "You can't help us agree on anything because we can't even agree on the color of the carpet in the hallway." You could then chunk up and say, "What's the purpose of your being in business? Is it to make a profit?" Both would likely have to agree with that. Subsequently, the idea that "we can't agree on anything" is immediately dissolved. By chunking up to a level of agreement, it is far easier to chunk back down and resolve the necessary issues. You've established, "So you can agree on some important things."

In negotiation, once you have chunked up for agreement, you would then only chunk back down again as you maintain agreement. Knowing what the big-picture outcome is, you can then use that to get final agreement. This is covered in the "conditional close" step to negotiating.

Precision Communication

A great tool to use for effective communication and negotiation, which will also help in the chunking process, is the Meta Model, also known as precision communication. The language of specificity is a framework to assist in clear and concise conveyance of ideas. It can be a highly effective tool in bridging the understanding divide.

In the early 1970s, Dr. Richard Bandler and John Grinder, founders of Neuro Linguistic Programming (NLP), set out to determine how change was created in a successful therapeutic interaction, and how we could replicate that change without going through years of therapy. They started by breaking down the patterns of the most effective therapists in the world at the time. The first was Virginia Satir.

Satir was known for her ability to speak with someone quite conversationally, and as she did, she would simply gain specificity through her language. By gaining this specificity, her patients would find that their problems would take on a different perspective. As a result, understanding between people was rapid and effective. Problems would melt away as the clients would gain clarity about their own unique rule book, and therefore the expectations and true meaning of their own and others' communication. An example of an interaction with Satir might go something like this:

Client: "He hurt me."
Virginia Satir: "How, specifically?"
Client: "Because he doesn't love me."

Virginia Satir: "How do you know he doesn't love you?"

Client: "Because when I come home he's always watching TV and not paying attention to me."

Virginia Satir: "How specifically does his watching TV mean that he doesn't love you?"

Client: "Well, I guess it doesn't necessarily mean that."

In this case, the client was able to see she had created a rule that in order for her to feel loved, she must be the center of attention all the time. That's not logical. No one can be the center of someone's attention *all* the time. But until the questions were asked, the client wasn't aware of this internal belief.

Precision communication is essential in negotiating. It is a linguistic model used to retrieve information from individuals by gaining specificity. It also serves to challenge the limits, or boundary conditions, of an individual's rule book and bring unconscious belief systems into awareness. If something is true for one person and not for another, you better believe it will hold up negotiations until the hidden beliefs behind a statement are put on the table and dealt with.

Precision communicating is a way of dealing with the deletions, distortions, and generalizations that we talked about in Chapter 4. Say, for example, that someone said, "Everyone always ignores my instructions." This is a generalization that has disempowered the individual and made him or her feel less confident. The words *everyone* and *always* represent the generalization that has been made. You may then ask, "Who specifically ignores your instructions?" "When specifically did they ignore them?" By using this simple technique, you can help that person gain awareness of limiting beliefs very quickly and easily.

Here is a systematic way of bringing anyone back to a more balanced perspective.

The basic questions used in precision communication are:

- What, specifically?
- How, specifically?
- When, specifically?
- Where, specifically?
- Who, specifically?

We go much deeper into precision communicating techniques in some of our trainings, but for now, start with the basic questions for specificity listed above.

Practice both the chunking techniques and precision communicating in your daily conversations and notice the difference it makes in understanding and rapport. You can even listen to other people's conversations to see whether the speaker is chunking up, down, or laterally. When you recognize how easily communication can stray off course or create misunderstandings due to people speaking from different chunking levels, you can then direct the conversation to first get everyone back on common ground, then arrive at any shared objectives.

Two other powerful ways of gaining specificity and reducing the room for error in communication are the following:

1. **Summation of points.** Sum up the communication by checking your understanding of what has been said. For example, "Let me just make sure I have complete understanding of where we are in this communication. You feel that we should approach the project in a way that is more conservative, is that correct?"
2. **Ask for feedback.** The other way to close a loop is to ask the receiver for feedback. For example, "So, based upon our discussion, what are you going to do differently, or how specifically do you plan on approaching this?"

The meaning of the communication is the response it elicits. If you are not getting the result you want, you are not communicating effectively. Change your approach until you get your objective. Using these various techniques will prove extremely helpful in determining the exact effect of your communication and keeping the flow of understanding moving between you and the other person.

Now you have the basic tools for powerful, persuasive communication—let the negotiations begin!

Pre-Negotiation Preparation

Negotiating is like traveling. Once you have determined your desired destination and before you've begun your trip, you map out the best route to get there. If you run into any impasses or detours along the way, you simply find alternative routes. All roads are somehow connected, so if you were to put your finger on one spot anywhere on the map and someone else had a finger on another, you could find countless ways to get from one to the other.

Before you can get to where you want to go, you always begin by preparing for your journey. The following five steps of preparation are essential before entering into any negotiations.

1. *Know your ideal outcome.* You have to first know exactly what you want before you can get it. So think ahead. Successful negotiation begins with successful planning. Before you set foot into any meeting, ask yourself what your best possible resolution or ideal outcome would be.

2. *Brainstorm all possible ways to arrive at this desired outcome.* Be flexible. Maintaining a fixed position negates any possibility of forward movement right off the bat. A fixed position can be a stuck position. This leads to frustration, and ultimately no one gets what they want. Explore your options. If there is more than one way (and there always is), then let your mind imagine all the alternatives. Whether you are negotiating for yourself or mediating between two people or groups, flexibility of thinking is a prerequisite.

A caveat to this is you also need to know before you utter your first word what you would absolutely not accept and what you would settle for. In other words, decide on the boundaries beyond which you will not go, as well as those lines you are willing to cross.

3. *Identify common goals.* While still in the prenegotiation stage, begin to look for areas on which both parties will probably agree. Once you have identified some common goals, you have your leverage. If negotiations ever begin to derail, you will be able to get things back on track by returning to these areas of alignment. These areas of potential agreement will be your basis for beginning the actual negotiations. For a true win-win resolution each party must have at least one shared desired outcome. Without common outcomes, there is no place to begin because there is no place to end that will satisfy both. Always presume that both sides can win!

4. *Recognize and plan for potential trouble spots.* Obviously there are areas of disagreement or you wouldn't be negotiating. So the key here is

to devise ways ahead of time that you could possibly approach and resolve those areas. This is where brainstorming all your alternative routes
to the ideal solution will come in handy. How you bring them up in discussion will also be important.

5. *Choose your best path to your ideal outcome.* Now that you have prepared yourself for every possible aspect of the coming negotiation, decide
which option you will present first. Even keep in mind the possibility that
none of the problems you have considered will present themselves and
that you may arrive at your win-win quicker than you thought.

Steps to Successful Negotiations

Once discussions begin, the most effective route to win-win solutions
follows these three stages:

Stage 1: Find Common Ground

1. *Establish rapport.* This should be the first step to any human interaction. However, it is especially useful in negotiating because it creates the much-needed atmosphere of responsiveness and trust that keeps
people working together toward a common vision.

2. *Clarify the agreed-upon outcome.* Have both sides state their goals.
If it seems there is little common ground, keep redefining what you really want and what that will mean to each party. Then pay close attention to the words used. We all use language differently, so it's possible
you do have shared goals yet state them differently. Listen for ideas you
can chunk up or down on to arrive at the common goal(s) you might not
have recognized. Again, you have no chance for resolution without common goals, so persist until you find some. Move on to the next step only
when you have clarified both sides' agreed-upon outcome.

3. *State a conditional close. Conditional close* is a term most often
used in sales. However, it is an invaluable tool for negotiating as it
quickly and invariably moves people closer to clarity, resolution, and
commitment. It's a linguistic device in which you simply ask someone
to suppose the desired outcome by using statements beginning, "Just
suppose . . ." or "If . . . then . . ."

For example, if you've just gotten both partners to agree that they are in business to make a profit, you then say, "So if we were able to get you profitable, then anyway we get you that would be okay?" Once both have agreed, the details of how they will become profitable become much simpler to resolve. If certain ways are not acceptable to either side, you've pinpointed the specific issues to solve up front.

If you are mediating between a chain of stores and their striking employees, and you have determined that both sides agree they want to get back to work to keep the company running, you could ask, "Just suppose we reached agreement on the outstanding issues, then would you agree to get back to work?" This is the most effective way to move through a stalemate because it reminds all parties of their shared objective to get the business up and running again. Conditional closes change people's focus from what they don't want to what they do want.

Stage 2: Move Beyond Differences

4. *Clarify areas to be resolved.* At this stage, not only are both sides united on common ground, but everyone also recognizes the common destination. The only question remaining is which route to take to get everyone there. It's time to clarify and highlight exactly what those roadblocks are.

5. *Uncover the intention behind areas of disagreement.* This is the most crucial and essential stage (and where negotiating is most fun), where you use your skills of chunking up and down to arrive at the true intention behind both sides' stated demands. For example, a workers union is in negotiations with management. The union says they want a higher hourly wage for their members. On probing, it is discovered that the reason for this is so that members will not have to work such long hours, because they want to spend more time with their families. By uncovering this intention, the management then has an option to satisfy the requirement without necessarily having to give the pay increase. They could, for example, give more vacation time, or move shifts around for those with families so they get to spend more time with their families. This step is very useful because it gets to the intent behind the request so that both parties can see that there might be a different way to meet their objectives. It requires you to probe by chunking up and asking, "And you want that for what purpose?"

6. *Chunk down while maintaining agreement.* Gradually chunk back down until you have returned to those specific areas that require resolution. Every time you reach disagreement, chunk back up until both sides agree. Then move back down through the trouble spots with the conditional close again, this time using more specific terms. For example, "If we got you (x,y,z), then any way you get that will be okay?" They will usually say yes because their focus is on the "what" more than the "how." Your job is the "how."

7. *Present options.* This is the point where you present some of the ways everyone could achieve the intention behind their original demands. They have already told you that they would accept any way that they could get their desired results, so anything you propose should be acceptable. Because you did your prenegotiation preparation, you will have several options up your sleeve to choose from. Get their ideas, too, and ask for their preferences. These will be the actual terms upon which you will soon find yourselves agreeing.

Stage 3: Resolution

8. *Confirm agreement.* Decide on the best option and move to close.

9. *Specify an action plan.* Now you are arriving at your common destination together. Summarize the detailed action plan, making sure you keep agreement through the details. Repeat steps 4 through 7 until both parties confirm resolution. End by confirming the first step you each need to take next.

You have just learned how to exquisitely handle any negotiations, whether you are negotiating your own contract, mediating for others as a business consultant, or sorting out differences within your own team or family. Combined with the win-win selling process, you now have all the steps you need to arrive at buying commitments in any context, whether buying into a proposal, a product, or a vision for the future. This will serve you well in leading people toward your vision with power and influence. That is what we will cover next.

16

How to Expand Your Sphere of Influence

Leadership appears to be the art of
getting others to want to do something
you are convinced should be done.

—Vance Packard

There are several laws and principles that when followed can assist you in creating maximum power and influence in your world. The first step you took was to expand your perspective of the world to increase your possibilities. Next you filled that broadened circle called "your game" with all the necessary mind-sets and strategies for success. Now you are developing other skills, or tricks of the trade, that will expand your sphere of influence as far as you choose to go in the world. As with all powerful information, these principles are open to abuse. The tools themselves are ethicless just as a scalpel can be used to heal or to harm. People have ethics. That is why I ask that you use these principles only to create win-win outcomes for you and those you work with. Being ecological in your actions is always the basic presupposed principle.

Cialdini's Principles

In his book *Influence: The Psychology of Persuasion*, Robert Cialdini pro-
poses six universal principles that are prevalent in human influence.
These include reciprocation, social validation, commitment and consistency, friendship and liking, authority, and scarcity. Cialdini discovered
these principles by studying human behavior in a number of situations
and noticing the major patterns of what makes people do the things
they do.

Reciprocity

Put in its simplest form, reciprocity is the need to address the balance. If
someone gives you something, there is an innate need or desire to return
the gift. This law works in some way in all relationships. If you have a
friendship and you always seem to give more to that friendship than you
receive, sooner or later the friendship will dissolve because there was not
a balanced give and take between you.

This technique is used widely in marketing with free gifts and
memberships, which hook the customer in and activate the law of reciprocity. Cialdini details how the Hare Krishnas used this law spectacu-
larly in the 1970s as a fundraising technique. They would give passersby
a flower. That's it! A harmless little flower. No money was requested.
However, this innate principle is so strong that even though the recipi-
ents didn't necessarily want the flower, the need to repay the debt of
kindness in some way resulted in the generation of millions of dollars.

Whatever you give out in life you tend to get back sooner or later.
So if you go through life looking for the good in others and helping
people get what they need and want, whether there is instant reward in
it or not, reciprocity will prevail somewhere along the line.

Social Validation

Cialdini refers to this law as social proof. This is simply the comfort and
acceptance that comes from seeing others do the same things we're doing. People are innately comforted if they are part of a pack. A feeling of
acceptance and belonging is gained from being like other people.

Again, marketers and salespeople have found ways to apply this law simply by adding testimonials from people "just like you" who have bought and loved their product. If you can make people feel comfortable and happy through your communication, then your results will reflect this. By activating the law of social proof you can make others feel at ease.

Commitment and Consistency

This is the need to remain consistent with an identity we have created for ourselves. Once we have been seen to make a decision or take a stand about something, we will experience pressure to behave consistently with that choice.

No one likes to admit they were wrong, and this is basically that premise taken to an extreme. Rather than admit a mistake, most people will maintain a particular course even though in their heart of hearts they know it is not the correct thing to do.

The world of marketing has tapped into this need by asking questions in sales that lead a person into the buying decision. This is not always a bad thing, but it is good to be aware of the power of these influencers so you can guard against their unscrupulous use. There are times where their use is valuable and will lead to win-win outcomes all around.

Take the time to understand what motivates other people and speak to them in their own language. This is why values elicitation is so useful. It can allow you to tap into a person's natural motivators and make a positive impact while also giving them what they need.

Friendship and Liking

This one is fairly obvious. You do business with people you like. This is why rapport skills are so imperative. The famous trial attorney Clarence Darrow once said, "The true job of a trial attorney is to get the jury to like their client."

In fact, in most courtroom situations the jury will make an initial evaluation and decision as to the guilt or innocence of the defendant within the first five minutes. All the information that comes in after that point will go to substantiate the decision they have already made about that person's guilt or innocence. The jurors will actually delete information that does not corroborate their initial decision.

Be someone you would like to be around. Have fun, laugh, be polite, friendly, and optimistic, and you'll be surprised how people will warm to you. If people like you they will listen to you. And if they listen, they may like what you have to propose.

Authority—The Power of Prestige

This is the sort of power a doctor wields in a white coat. We place huge importance on information given by authority figures. The level of trust that is given to them often seems to bypass the individual's need to validate that authority.

We are accustomed to listening and responding to people of authority and are, therefore, apt to alter our behavior as a result of a suggestion from them. Marketers have used this to great effect by getting celebrity endorsement or testimonials from so-called qualified professionals. For example, health supplements may be endorsed by a famous athlete and accompanied by a testimonial from a leading nutritionist.

Hypnosis uses a concept called the *prestige suggestion*. A prestige suggestion is any suggestion accepted by someone simply because of the level of prestige of the person who delivered it. Ninety percent of hypnosis is prestige. People will often follow the suggestions simply because they are delivered by "a hypnotist." It works the same way in the field of medicine. You have heard, no doubt, of the placebo effect. This is a result of the prestige suggestion that comes from the doctor and the apparent legitimacy of the medication provided. The more prestige or authority we acquire, the more our interpersonal suggestions and communications will be heeded.

In the 19th century, Franz Anton Mesmer became famous for his ability to heal sick or diseased people by mesmerizing them. He was so successful that at one point, thousands of people a day were coming to see him. He would pass his hands over them, their eyes would roll back in their heads, and they would go into convulsions. Then they would be healed. This worked very well for him until a commission was empowered by the politicians and the doctors in an attempt to debunk him and prove him a fake. Three people served on this commission: the French chemist Lavoisiere, a French specialist in pain control named Guillotine, and the American Benjamin Franklin. Mesmer claimed to heal people through a magnetic energy that flowed forth from his hands. In his report back to the French government, Benjamin Franklin said, "I cannot see this mesmeric energy of which he speaks, and therefore, he must be a fake." As a result, Mesmer lost his prestige and authority, and many of the people who he had previously healed became sick again. This story is not only a reminder of the power of authority but the power of beliefs.

Scarcity

Here's a paradox of life: The principle of social validation states that we feel comfort if other people are doing what we are doing. In other words, there is safety in numbers. Yet the principle of scarcity says we are also influenced by the need to be different—to stand out from the crowd!

An opportunity will always seem more valuable if there is an element of scarcity to it. Open any magazine and see the words "Limited offer—must close Sunday!" or "Limited edition collector's item—only two left!" The feeling that we may miss out on something special and unique will drive us to take action.

These are some of the hallmarks of powerful communication, so understand their innate ability to influence and bring them into your communication when appropriate. As you continue to expand your game, you will need to enroll the efforts of other players on your team to reach your objectives. Life is not a solo sport, even though many of us would like to think it could be. It involves assisting others to achieve their dreams too. This requires vision and leadership and the ability to shift perceptions through the creative use of language.

17

CHAPTER

The Art of Spin and Masterful Storytelling: How to Shift Perceptions through Language

Learning the game of power requires a certain way of looking at the world, a shifting of perspective.

—**Robert Greene**

When I was younger, I traveled all over the world—to Mexico, where I rode horses through the desert; to Greece and Turkey, where I saw wondrous, underwater sunken cities. I explored caves in the Italian islands and the British West Indies. I went wreck diving in St. Barts and shark feeding in Tahiti. I was always interested in seeing the world from every possible viewpoint. It was this that excited me, because I was always so curious as to how to see things differently. Seeing new things instantaneously provides new reference points. That is why telling great stories using vivid imagery is one of the fastest, most effective ways to alter people's points of view. People tend to think of others as natural storytellers. But this, too, is a learnable skill. I break down the process into specific steps that eventually can become so natural it is artful. Stories can be profoundly magic, as we know from going to the movies. Before detailing this powerful technique for expanding people's perceptions, let's talk about shifting their viewpoints while getting a point across with the art of spin.

The term *spin* has gotten a somewhat negative spin put on it due to some of the people who perhaps use and abuse it. However, the art of spin is simply shifting the frame of perception around something to alter the evaluation of it. Spin, to some extent, is the human manifestation of what we talked about at the beginning of the book—the universe changes based on who and what is looking at it.

An event is not inherently good or bad, right or wrong. Judgments and evaluations we make about events are subjective, based completely upon our individual model of the world. Because no two people have exactly the same model of the world, people's interpretations of outside events can't help but be biased. The observer always and intimately affects what is observed.

Mother Teresa received criticism for feeding the hungry instead of teaching them how to feed themselves. According to the critics, she was therefore doing the hungry a disservice by feeding them. Theirs is a fair and valid opinion. Many, if not most, of the people in the world would say she was doing them a huge service, which is also a fair and valid belief. The event did not change, just the perspective on the event and how it was spun. The world of Mother Teresa was viewed very differently depending on who was looking at it.

Spin is a relatively new term and is used frequently in politics and marketing. A great example of political spin occurred in the presidential primary debates between Walter Mondale and Ronald Reagan. At the time, Mondale was pushing the point that Reagan was too old to run for president. At one point in the debate, the moderator asked Reagan if he thought that age should be made an issue in the debate. Reagan replied, "No. I don't think it should be an issue. I refuse to make an issue of my opponent's youth and inexperience."

This was a fantastic use of spin—he turned the whole argument on its head and, rather than defend his age, he used the same line from a different angle. He targeted his opponent's "youth and inexperience," which shifted the frame of reference, therefore turning an attack around to be utterly ineffective.

Henry Kissinger once opened a press conference by saying, "Who has the questions to the answers I've prepared?" his point being that he was a master of delivering the message he intended to deliver. No matter how a question was posed, he could turn it around to his advantage. Although the term *spin* has more recently been given a somewhat negative *spin*, it is just another word for reframing, or offering a new perspective.

S.P.I.N. P.A.T.T.E.R.N.S.

An easy acronym to remember when using persuasive language is S.P.I.N. P.A.T.T.E.R.N.S., explained in a moment. There are many linguistic patterns that we can use to assist us in changing people's perceptions. Why would we want to shift someone's perception, you might ask. Well, would you like to know how to assist people to see your perspective? Or to take up a cause? Would you like to make your point hit home at a company meeting? What if you could respond to any objection or argument and persuade people to see things differently? Consciously or not, some of our greatest leaders have used these techniques, including Dr. Martin Luther King Jr. and Nelson Mandela.

Here are twelve different patterns that can totally change the way people view anything:

1. S: Shift to a larger frame.
2. P: Perspective of others.
3. I: Importance of higher values.
4. N: Negative consequences.
5. P: Point out a higher level of abstraction.
6. A: Analogy or metaphor.
7. T: Transcend the generalization.
8. T: Turn to another issue.
9. E: Evaluation.
10. R: Reversal.
11. N: Newly define.
12. S: Separate intention from behavior.

Let's take two separate beliefs or opinions and see how we would use each of the spin patterns to help the person see that belief from another perspective. I will repeat the following two statements as examples and offer possible responses to them for each type of spin pattern:

a. "I'll never be successful because I have a learning disability."
b. "I can't take your seminar because it's too expensive."

S. Shift to a Larger Frame

To generate this spin pattern, it's important to realize that for people to hold the belief or generalization they currently have, they must be looking at the event or belief through a certain size of frame. By widening the frame size to include things they were not previously aware of or have not yet noticed, you can change the meaning of the event or belief within their thinking. A simple way to do this is to ask yourself, "What is a larger frame or something they haven't noticed, which, when noticed, will cause their position to change?" Here are some ways to spin these objections:

a. "I'll never be successful because I have a learning disability."

   Response: "You're just saying that because you haven't re-searched all the people with similar challenges who have be-come massively successful."

b. "I can't take your seminar because it's too expensive."

   Response: "Once you've taken a look at our tuition financing options, you'll understand how affordable it can really be."

P. Perspective of Others

Remember that no two people share the same model of the world. To al-ter another person's perspective, you need to recognize any generaliza-tion and show how it could be viewed differently, from another's perspective. Apply these responses to the same two objections:

a. "I'll never be successful because I have a learning disability."

   Response: "Many people—myself included—don't believe in learning disabilities . . . just in ineffective learning strategies. And learning strategies can be changed."

b. "I can't take your seminar because it's too expensive."

   Response: "Our graduates understand that what was really ex-pensive was the time they wasted before gaining the insights in our program."

I. Importance of Higher Values

Events have no inherent meaning until they are passed through an indi-vidual's rule book, as we discussed earlier. Values are one of the major factors in our interpretation of events. During the Monica Lewinsky scandal, two political parties, representing different sets of nationally held values, were viewing the same situation and placing a different meaning on it. One of the effective spin patterns used throughout the course of the scandal by President Clinton and the Democratic Party was that of the *importance of higher values.* Wasn't it *more important* to get back to the work of the country? To be forgiving as a people? Wasn't it *more important* that he was such an effective president, and wasn't the great state of the economy *more important* than what occurred in his personal life? According to them, within their values system, it was.

The way to tap into the power of the higher values pattern is to figure out the individual's relevant values and then ask, "What is a higher universally held value?" or "What is a higher held value for the individual I'm communicating with that, when brought to his or her awareness, would result in a change in meaning?" Using the same example, here is a way to respond by using a higher value:

a. "I'll never be successful because I have a learning disability."
   Response: "Isn't it more important to believe in yourself than to create reasons or excuses for your lack of success?"
b. "I can't take your seminar because it's too expensive."
   Response: "Aren't you worth investing in?"

N. Negative Consequences

Shift the attention to the negative consequences of holding on to the generalization. This alters the person's perception. For example:

a. "I'll never be successful because I have a learning disability."
   Response: "It's beliefs like that that keep people from ever rising above their challenges."
b. "I can't take your seminar because it's too expensive."
   Response: "What's it going to cost you if you don't do it? What is the price—physically, emotionally and financially?"

P. Point Out a Higher Level of Abstraction

This pattern can be utilized to bring into the person's mind exaggerated or larger patterns.

a. "I'll never be successful because I have a learning disability."
   Response: "Many people have excuses for not succeeding in

life. For some it's their sex, race, or creed, and for others it's a challenge such as yours. It's not that successful people don't have challenges. Successful people rise above their challenges."

b. "I can't take your seminar because it's too expensive."
Response: "Thoughts like that serve only to keep people from learning the tools that can change their lives for the better."

A. Analogy or Metaphor

Answer the generalization, objection, or event with an appropriate analogy or a metaphor.

a. "I'll never be successful because I have a learning disability."
Response: "I used to think it took me longer to learn things than most people, and it was that very belief that caused me to work even harder and propel myself on to greater success."

b. "I can't take your seminar because it's too expensive."
Response: "Jon Andre Bliss said the same thing, but then he realized it was too expensive not to do it. He attended the course and within 30 days he had virtually tripled his sales."

T. Transcend the Generalization

This pattern could also be called "breaking the generalization." Shift attention to a time or situation when the person's generalization was not true.

a. "I'll never be successful because I have a learning disability."
Response: "Richard Branson was told he was dyslexic, and that didn't stop him from becoming a billionaire."

b. "I can't take your seminar because it's too expensive."
Response: "Too expensive compared to what? Compared to the cost of not having this information? You pay for education once. You pay for ignorance over and over again."

T. Turn to Another Issue

Bring to the individual's attention what you believe to be the key issue. This pattern is frequently used in politics. When Al Gore asked for a recount of the Florida votes and was first granted it, he said, "It's not a victory for Al Gore, but a victory for our democracy."

a. "I'll never be successful because I have a learning disability."
Response: "The issue isn't whether you *can* become successful; the issue is whether you *are willing* to become successful despite the challenges you're confronted with."

b. "I can't take your seminar because it's too expensive."
Response: "The issue isn't the amount of the investment. The issue is how much you think you're worth investing in."

E. Evaluation

People make their own evaluations based on their model of the world and then label circumstances as meaning one thing or another. This pattern will allow them to see their own assumptions, then alter their interpretation and consider new possibilities.

a. "I'll never be successful because I have a learning disability."
Response: "Your success is not determined by your challenges. Your success is determined by your commitments."

b. "I can't take your seminar because it's too expensive."
Response: "The price of the seminar doesn't mean you can't attend, it simply means you've got to commit yourself to your own success. Where there's a will there's a way."

R. Reversal

Utilize their reasoning to show them that the very reason they gave the objection is the same reason they should take the action you prescribe. This pattern is used quite frequently in sales. When someone says, "It costs too much, I can't afford it," the salesperson responds with, "That's why you have to do it."

a. "I'll never be successful because I have a learning disability."
Response: "That's exactly why you need to become successful—so you can prove to yourself and others how powerful you can be when you decide to overcome something."

b. "I can't take your seminar because it's too expensive."
Response: "That's exactly why you need to do whatever you have to in order to attend. How long do you want to go on not being able to afford the things you really want in life?"

N. Newly Define

This pattern gives an alternate definition they may not have thought about, and thereby opens their eyes to a different way of seeing something, or redefines their perceptions.

    a. "I'll never be successful because I have a learning disability."
    Response: "Success is not something that is achieved by having no challenges. Success is the process of overcoming your challenges."
    b. "I can't take your seminar because it's too expensive."
    Response: "Our program is not expensive, it's valuable. How much would you pay for something that helped you to double your income? That's exactly what Christine Winters did after attending."

S. Separate Intention from Behavior

This pattern is used to separate intention from behavior so that it's easy to see where one is not supporting the other.

    a. "I'll never be successful because I have a learning disability."
    Response: "I know your intention is to keep yourself from experiencing disappointment, but how disappointed would you be if you got to the end of your life and you never reached your full potential because of that lousy excuse?"
    b. "I can't take your seminar because it's too expensive."
    Response: "I know that you're interested in making wise financial decisions and we've got lots of clients that will assure you this is one of the smartest financial decisions you could make."

These spin patterns are some of the fastest and most effective ways to influence others positively. I have a lot of fun with these because using language in this way, with the people's best interest in mind, I can watch the instant change that occurs within their minds. Their limited perspective is expanded and they see clearly how much more is possible than they previously imagined. With your developed sensory acuity, you can almost literally watch people's thinking begin to change direction. The best responses cause individuals to reflect on the assumptions and beliefs implicit in the words they choose. Whether you are going to an investor for a business loan or talking with your teenager, instead of dreading objections to your proposal, you can now look at responses from others as a wide-open opportunity to expand their thinking. You can practically see their minds ticking after that, wondering what else is possible too.

Stories and Masterful Metaphors

People need stories more than bread itself.
They tell us how to live and why.

—Arabian Nights

Stories and metaphors are another powerful way of expressing your ideas, teaching, and assisting people to see the world in new ways. Storytelling is an essential tool in getting a team moving forward congruently toward the accomplishment of noble objectives. The best teachers of all time have been able to communicate in ways that simplify grand ideas by conveying their message through some other event or situation. Some of the greatest social movements that have ever graced the planet have been accomplished with the help of charismatic leaders who knew the power of communicating through metaphor and analogy. Martin Luther King Jr. was one such leader who possessed this power of persuasive storytelling. There are also leaders within the world of business who have made a tremendous impact on people using metaphor.

Warren Buffett's primary mentor, Benjamin Graham, the grandfather of value investing, used the now famous metaphor of Mr. Market to explain how to be an outstanding investor in an unpredictable market. He said to imagine that as an investor, you are in business with a manic-depressive partner who goes through huge mood swings on a daily basis. One moment he's telling you business is great and he quotes you a price for which he's willing to buy you out. A few hours later his sunny outlook disappears and he's all gloom and doom, trying to tell you your company is now worth next to nothing so you should sell immediately, while you still can. The best time to buy is actually when he's overly pessimistic and desperate to sell, not when he's being overly optimistic, when everyone else is buying. To this day Buffett often recalls the story of Mr. Market when making investment decisions, especially if he's ever tempted to get fearful and sell when others are fearful.

Children's books and movies are also full of important life lessons presented as metaphors wrapped within the plots and story lines. Walt Disney movies are well known for this. Take for example the movie *The Lion King*. A young lion cub named Simba is playing outside the safe area. Simba gets into trouble and his father goes to the rescue, only to be killed himself by a stampeding herd of wildebeest.

Feeling he is to blame for his father's death, the distraught Simba runs away from the pride in shame. He goes off to live with other animals in a faraway part of the forest. Several years later a childhood friend of Simba's comes and tells him that an evil tyrannical leader has taken charge of the pride and Simba is the only one who can defeat him. When she asks Simba to return, Simba says that he can never return because of what happened in the past. One of Simba's newfound friends, a wise old sage and monkey named Rafiki, goes to speak with him.

"Why can you not go back and take your rightful place?" asks Rafiki. Simba sadly replies that he can't change the past.

At that point, Rafiki raps Simba across the head with his walking stick. Simba yelps in pain and demands, "What was that for?"

Rafiki replies, "It does not matter—it's in the past." He then attempts to hit Simba again, but this time Simba ducks. Now he understands Rafiki's message: We can't change the past, but we can learn the lessons and teachings from it so that we can change our behaviors in the future to produce the results that we want. The purpose of past experience is not to limit us, but rather to teach and instruct us—a profound lesson presented within a wonderfully evocative children's tale.

The Purpose of Stories and Metaphors

The main purpose of storytelling is to bypass conscious resistance to hearing the point that is being made or taught. Because everyone comes into any conversation with their own set of ideas and meanings, it is sometimes difficult to get people to see a certain perspective because they are emotionally attached to their existing one.

By dissociating the individual or group from a given situation, it is possible to lead them to a solution for a particular problem or situation without implicating or blaming anyone. That's what happens therapeutically with a story. It works well, because when people are stuck in a problem they tend to have quite a bit of feeling and energy invested in it. When you walk up to someone like that and say, "Here's your solution," it's usually not very effective. But if you can represent the issue the individual is currently experiencing by means of a seemingly unrelated experience, you can open up a neural pathway that can lead to a new point of view and better understanding. The person hearing the story may or may not consciously get the connection between the story and his or her own experience. Nonetheless, they often go on to make the necessary internal shifts and solve the problem anyway. From a Neurological Repatterning™ point of view, what you are doing is creating new neural networks inside the individual, which lead ultimately to new ways of viewing their relationship to the world and, therefore, new behavior.

Analogies

An analogy is used to simplify communication by drawing a relationship between two things that had no prior relationship. It can assist someone to see a similarity between something they are already familiar with and something they are not. This makes them more comfortable with and able to relate to or better understand any idea you are trying to get across. It can also be used like a story to drive home a point or to assist people to see things in new ways.

The key to making an analogy work is to go from the known to the unknown. When Jesus spoke of making his disciples "fishers of men," that was an example of a superb analogy that allowed his audience to bridge the gap between what they already understood (fishing) and what they didn't (their purpose). An analogy gets your listeners to transfer their positive associations with what's familiar to the vision or information you're relaying.

After studying many of the most influential communicators of all time, I have found one of the most eloquent and inspirational to be Dr. Martin Luther King, Jr. Note the use of analogy in this excerpt from Dr. King's famous "I Have a Dream" speech:

> *In a sense we have come to our nation's capitol to cash a check. When the architects of our republic wrote the magnificent words of the*

*Constitution and the Declaration of Independence, they were sign-
ing a promissory note to which every American was to fall heir. This
note was a promise that all men would be guaranteed the inalien-
able rights of life, liberty, and the pursuit of happiness.*

*It is obvious today that America has defaulted on this promis-
sory note insofar as her citizens of color are concerned. Instead of
honoring this sacred obligation, America has given the Negro people
a bad check—a check which has come back marked "insufficient
funds." But we refuse to believe that the bank of justice is bankrupt.
We refuse to believe that there are insufficient funds in the great
vaults of opportunity of this nation. So we have come to cash this
check—a check that will give us upon demand the riches of freedom
and the security of justice.*

Analogies work best when they meet one of two criteria: They are
either (1) universal experiences, meaning that anybody can relate to
them, or (2) tailor-designed for the individual based on that person's interests and values.

I was once working with a nine-year-old boy who had been
branded as having Attention Deficit Hyperactivity Disorder (ADHD).
I'll call the boy Jonathan for the purposes of this story. Jonathan's parents had tried everything to calm him down and get him to pay attention
in class, to no avail. They called me in to work with him, and I showed
up at his house to meet him one day. When I met Jonathan, he really
was bouncing off the walls. He would switch from topic to topic as he
spoke incessantly. His shoes were off, so I took mine off too, and then I
began to match and mirror his overt physiology. Once I had sufficient
rapport, I slowed down and then noticed that he began to follow my
lead and slow down himself.

At this point, I asked him about how he did in school. "I don't do
very well, because I have ADHD," he replied. I asked him what he really
liked and enjoyed doing when he was not at school. He told me that he
loved to do gymnastics. When I asked him to tell me more about that,
his physiology and energy changed dramatically. His focus shifted completely, and for the first time since I had begun speaking with him he was
able to stay on topic. He told me about various competitions he had
been in and how much he loved it. So then I asked him about how he

learned to do gymnastics, and he continued with much pride and excitement to describe the process. Then I commented on *how much fun it sounded to learn* and began to assist him in linking learning to fun through our conversation.

One thing I notice with children who are labeled ADHD is that they seem to be able to pay attention to things that they like and enjoy. It's often only when they don't like something or they lack commitment to something that they exhibit unruly behavior. There is no such thing as lack of attention. We are always paying attention to something, although it may not be what others want us to focus on. I asked Jonathan what else he really enjoyed doing, and he mentioned that he liked to sit on his deck and watch the dolphins in the ocean. So the two of us went up on the deck and watched the dolphins together. Once again his focus and attention were fixated. I explained to him, while we sat there, how easy it was to really focus in on things. We went back inside and I asked him if he would like to learn how to keep the teachers off his back, get better grades, make his classes at school go by a lot faster, and be able to spend more time doing gymnastics instead of homework.

He let me know that would suit him just fine. Then I taught him how to go into the learning state (the state of expanded awareness you learned earlier). I told him it was similar to dolphin watching. Just like he was watching a dolphin in the ocean, he could focus on a spot just above eye level and then allow his vision to expand out into the peripheral. He went swiftly and easily into the learning state, and soon it became quite easy for him to slow down and focus anytime he chose.

At the end of our time together, I explained that whenever he wanted to, he could simply go into the learning state; then his class time would pass by very quickly, the information being taught in class would just go right inside his head, and he would remember everything easily. The learning state in this case serves as a type of waking hypnotic trance, which is quite useful to choose to go into for the purpose of learning and retaining information.

By transferring the fun of learning gymnastics—something he was quite familiar with—to learning in general, he was able to experience something beyond the belief instilled in him that he wasn't good at learning. The analogy of watching a dolphin made it easier for Jonathan to focus and pay attention. What makes the analogy work is to go from the known to the unknown. In this particular case, it also provided new resources that Jonathan didn't know he had.

How to Create Stories

The construction of stories can range from simplistic to quite complex, yet regardless of the level of complexity they can be incredibly powerful in solving problems for others or assisting them to think about things in new ways.

In order to construct a story, all that is necessary is to find a situation or circumstance that parallels the concept you'd like to illustrate. For the purposes of explaining overall story construction, I will describe how to create one in the context of creating behavioral change. This will help you better understand the intricacies of designing metaphors that can have an incredible impact on the consciousness of the other person. With this deeper understanding of the process of story construction, you can take the patterns taught here and apply them cross-contextually in business, leadership, sales, activism, coaching, or education.

Constructing a Story to Create Change or Get Someone to Take Action

There are four basic steps in this type of story construction:

1. Find out what the problem or current situation is, and determine in your own mind the solution. It is also beneficial at this point to determine what is preventing the other person from finding the solution.
2. Chunk up on the problem or current situation (in the same way you learned in the Negotiating section in Chapter 15). Ask yourself, "What is this situation an example of?"
3. Chunk laterally by asking yourself, "What are other examples of this?"
4. Using one of these examples, tell a story about someone or something in a similar situation who resolved the problem or discovered resources they didn't realize they had. An alternative is to end the story with the negative consequences of not taking action.

You can create change within individuals, on both a thinking and behavioral level, and ultimately get them to take a desired action using story. Let's take a closer look at each step of the process of story construction.

What Is the Problem?

The first step is to find out what the problem state or current situation is, then determine the best possible solution. Either ask the person directly or ask yourself, "Where are they now? And where would they like to be instead?" Once you understand the issue, it's important to connect closely to it in yourself so that you are able to fully appreciate the situation and come up with a story that will deeply affect the listener in a way that will cause them to more easily solve their own problem.

Let's say, for example, that you know someone who wants to increase his business, but feels he can't really expand because he believes he doesn't have the money it would take. You know it's necessary for him to think outside the box of his current thinking in order to come up with some creative financing solutions. This solution may be better delivered in a story. Some people will undoubtedly ask, "If you already know the solution, why not just tell the person straight out?" When you use a story, the person is prompted to search for his own meaning and to come to the solution in his own mind. This makes the process inductive, which is far more powerful than simply handing him the solution. He arrives at the solution himself, and therefore is more likely to act on it.

What Is This Problem an Example Of?

The second step of the process is to chunk up on the problem or current situation. The idea is to get more abstract on the essence of the stated quandary. To see the problem in a bigger context, ask yourself, "What is this current problem an example of?" It could be an example of "feeling stuck" or "without options." It could also be an example of "rigid thinking" or "lack of creative ideas." In this step, your job is to pick the concept you chunk up to that you feel most closely resembles the nature of the issue. In this case, let's say you decided that the problem is an example of "feeling stuck." Then you would ask yourself the question:

Where Are There Parallel Examples of This Problem?

The third step now is to chunk laterally, or think of examples that would demonstrate the larger concept at which you arrived. In this case, after chunking up to "feeling stuck," the next question to ask is, "What are some *other* examples of feeling stuck?" It needs to be something the listener can relate to that would also be useful to lead the listener to a powerful solution. In this case, it could be traffic, being stuck on the freeway, standing in a line at a busy amusement park that isn't moving, or even a business story of someone else you know who was in a similar situation that ended positively. There are plenty of answers other than those, by the way. These were simply the ones that came to mind.

Tell a Parallel Story to Solve the Problem

The final step of the process of story construction is to create the story—using one of the examples that you created from step three, find a scenario that bridges the gap between the problem and the solution. Remember, the key to an effective outcome is using a character who either solves the problem within the story or discovers necessary resources he didn't know he had that can enable him to reach his goal. While it is not absolutely necessary, the story is most effective when the person can immediately see the correlations between his or her situation and the story. For those who don't like to be told what to do or think, you can make your story more abstract so that they don't quite make the connection consciously. The higher you chunk up to abstraction in your story, the more deeply unconscious the story's effect is. Let's look at how the process breaks down for this last example.

A person you are helping tells you he's frustrated because he wants to increase his business but he believes he can't expand because he doesn't have the marketing dollars it would take. You use the four steps of story construction as follows:

1. Problem or current situation: "Can't grow business." Solution: Think outside the box.
2. The situation is an example of feeling stuck.
3. Other examples of feeling stuck: standing in a long line at an amusement park, a car stuck in traffic, someone in a similar situation who increased their business.
4. Story told: Richard Branson growing Virgin Airlines.

Here is a story that I could tell to this person. I have italicized the words that I might emphasize while telling it.

Richard Branson, founder of the Virgin Companies, didn't have much of a marketing budget when he launched Virgin Airlines. And he *felt a bit stuck at the time*, because he knew that he needed to get the word out about the new airline. So one day he was *desperately trying to figure out what to do*, and he stopped and said to himself, "*No problem is insurmountable. You can do this. You've just got to think outside the box.*" Now, he knew that publicity, which can often be free, was worth many times the value of advertising, so he decided to *find a way* to get the publicity without paying the advertising dollars. Branson did it with a transatlantic crossing in the Virgin Challenger boat in an attempt to beat the speed record, which he failed on his first attempt. Nonetheless, the publicity that was created was enormous, which drove many people to his new airline. Although not everyone is that extreme, *certainly thinking outside of the box can lead to new solutions* that perhaps didn't even exist as possibilities to a mind that wasn't searching for them.

The Distinctions That Make Stories Work

Many features can cause a story to work or to make an impact in someone's thinking, and therefore have the potential of affecting or changing behavior. The first and most important aspect is that the story must be intimately linked to that person's values. By constructing and delivering a story that holds importance to the person or group you're communicating with, you will captivate their attention.

Other distinctions we can add to the construction of stories to add impact are as follows:

- Create a direct relationship between a character or characters in the story and the person or persons you are communicating with.
- If possible use real-life people, objects, or circumstances familiar to the person you are communicating with. Anything that adds familiarity within the story will draw them in and assist them to connect with it. In Dr. King's famous speech, he compared racial inequality to the writing of a bad check.

- Use a story that relates to something that holds significance to the person. Jesus spoke to the fishermen about becoming fishers of men.
- Use embedded commands and direct quotes inside the context of the story to ensure important points stand out, or to deliver a specific message. Using a direct quote delivers a message to the person through a character in the story. For example, in the preceding Branson story, where Branson says to himself, "No problem is insurmountable. You can do this. You've just got to think outside the box," the direct quote can be delivered lower and louder, with tonal emphasis, so that it stands out from the rest of the story, making the most impact on the listener. A direct command is one given overtly, such as "Close the door." This type of command can also be hidden or embedded within a question or a statement to soften the commanding aspect, but to nevertheless deliver a specific message that stands out in the mind of the person or group with whom you are communicating. An example would be, "I'm wondering if someone could *close the door*," the final part of the statement being delivered in a lower voice and with tonal emphasis.
- Remember, you do not have to provide the solution outright in the story or explain the meaning of your story. Instead, you may sometimes want to leave it open enough to cause the person or group to search for the meaning and come to their own solutions. This can be quite powerful, as they will still be making new connections long after you have told it. They may also make associations you never even thought of—so it's often very advantageous to leave it up to them.

CHAPTER

Golden Rules for Success

It is impossible for a man to conceal himself. In every act, word or gesture he stands revealed as he is, and not as he would have himself appear to be. From the Universe, nothing is or can be hidden.

—Ernest Holmes

We talked about chunking earlier and the importance of learning to think in various levels of abstraction. I firmly believe that the most abstract foundation of success is communication. If you are a master communicator, if you can excite, inspire, and motivate yourself and others, then your success is assured. Part 3 of this book has been dedicated to giving you some of the most powerful techniques available anywhere in the world so that you can become a masterful communicator.

Think about it for a second. You can't not communicate. From the moment you were born, you have been communicating all the time. Even as a baby, without language, you made yourself understood through a myriad of emotions, facial expressions, sounds, and body language. Communication is a primary tool you use to navigate through life. The most successful people in history, regardless of your definition of success, have been masterful communicators able to inspire and motivate others, challenge paradigms, and change the world.

What Are You Communicating?

Everything you do, don't do, say, or don't say is communicating something to the world around you. If you arrive late to a meeting, that action has communicated something about who you are, whether it's a fair assumption or not. If you are overweight, that visual representation communicates something about who you are, whether it's true or not. If you smoke, that activity communicates something about who you are, whether you intend it to or not.

The purpose here is not to judge what you choose to do. It is to make you see that *everything* you say and do is communicating something to the outside world about your character, your values, your intentions, and about what your boundaries are and what you are willing to accept in your life.

Once you understand this, you can make your own judgment about whether something is an accurate reflection of your character or not. You can even make a choice that, though it may not be, you wish to continue to do it anyway for whatever reason. Don't be fooled—communication is so much more than what you say.

One of the things that I have learned from my personal experience as well as from studying the most influential communicators of all time is the importance of character. In terms of creating long-term relationships, your character will eventually be communicated to the people with whom you interact through your consistent actions.

As Coach John Wooden of UCLA once said, "Be more concerned with your character than your reputation. Your reputation is merely who people think you are, your character is who you really are." It is therefore important to project your character and guard your reputation. What you communicate to the world reveals your character. This book is about providing you with the best information that will allow you to dramatically change your experience of the world and produce the results you want. How you use the tools depends on your character. Whether you are building a business, a nation, a family, or a relationship with your team, the way you treat others and interact consistently with them will determine your long-term success.

This chapter is a roundup of all the golden rules—character traits and practices that can make your success long-lasting. A strong character serves as the strongest foundation on which to build a legacy.

Your Map Is Not Their Territory

One of the keys to communication excellence is to understand that people's ideas of the world are different. Another person's map of the world is often referred to as their model of the world—the unique way they perceive and shape experience. Because people have different backgrounds, values, upbringings, life experiences, and reference points, they will have a model of the world that is entirely their own and unlike anybody else's. Dr. Milton Erickson said that a person's model of the world is as "unique as his or her thumbprint." Yet when we speak to each other we assume that what we are trying to convey and what is being interpreted are the same thing.

Communication is about respecting others and assisting them to understand what you are trying to say. In order to do that, you must learn to walk in their shoes and speak to them in their language.

A great example of this is written up in a study of Dr. Milton Erickson's work called *Phoenix*, by David Gordon and Maribeth Meyers-Anderson. The book includes a case history of a six-year-old boy who was sucking his thumb incessantly. His parents, who were both psychologists, tried everything they knew to get him to quit, but to no avail. Finally, they decided to bring him to see Dr. Erickson, the famous psychiatrist and master communicator. Dr. Erickson sat in his office with the boy and his parents. He looked across at the young boy with his thumb in his mouth, and then began to speak. "Your parents have brought you here so that I would get you to stop sucking your thumb." The boy looked defiantly at him, all the while continuing to suck his thumb.

"But I don't have any right to tell you to stop it. Little six-year-old boys have every right in the world to suck their thumbs, because that's what six-year-old little boys do." The boy seemed to be pleased with this response as he looked victoriously at each of his parents while he continued to suck his thumb. Dr. Milton Erickson continued, "Of course, a grown-up seven-year-old would never suck his thumb because a seven-year-old is a young man. And a grown-up seven-year-old young man would never suck his thumb like a six-year-old little boy." The little boy stopped sucking his thumb a couple of months before his seventh birthday!

In this example, Dr. Erickson didn't attempt to use adult logic to change the little boy's behavior. Instead, he respected the child's model of the world and used it to assist him in wanting to change himself. In the little boy's model of the world, wanting to be a grown-up seven-year-old young man was important to him, so stopping the behavior was logical and the obvious thing for him to do.

Communication Can Only Be Deemed Successful When You Get the Outcome You Desire

Communication is a complex issue, but essentially what you are creating in your reality right now is simply the result of your communication up to this point. If you are not getting the results that you want in your life, then chances are you are not communicating what you want to the world in a way that is understood. It is likely that your actions are communicating something very different than your words.

This is one reason why we went through the process of revealing your unconscious rule book earlier. Before you can communicate congruently with anyone about what you want, your words and actions must be conveying the same message. For example, you could be frustrated that your employees continue to spend excessively even after you have told them at meetings on several occasions that it is important to keep expenses down. You may assume that they're not listening to you, because your words are not having the deterrent effect on them that you wanted. However, the extravagant company holiday party that you hosted communicated loud and clear to them that it's okay to be excessive. It may be that one of your unconscious values is approval, and the company party fulfilled that value, but that same value is in conflict with your value of being frugal. This misalignment in your values manifests itself in unclear communication; it also makes your company's success vulnerable to the results of spending at a level you cannot actually afford. Your actions will reveal what is truly important to you, even if you aren't consciously aware of it yourself.

Until you can communicate congruently, internally as well as externally, about what you want, you will always feel as though you are taking two steps forward and three steps back. What you say, how you behave, and what you do must all be in alignment with your dreams in order for them to become a reality.

Treat People As You Would Like to Be Treated

We have all heard the biblical rule, "Do unto others as you would have done unto you." It is without a doubt as relevant today as it was when first spoken. Sometimes, in our haste to get through the day and get to our destination, we forget that the people we are dealing with are just like us. They have their good days and bad days, they have their concerns and fears and deadlines just as we do. They would like to laugh and feel good about what they do, just as we would.

As well as being one of the most important human relations principles of all time, the golden rule is also worth considering for the karmic effect of your actions. Whatever you dish out to the world will always come back around. Everything must be answered for and every debt must be cleared before we can learn the lessons that will allow us to move on to our next level of achievement.

Don't Make a Practice of Burning Bridges

I remember one day speaking with my friend Alejandro Ophilia, who once was the Chilean Ambassador to the United States and China. Alejandro said, "One thing that I've learned in my life and my career is to never, ever burn bridges." Some of my most important lessons in life that resulted in my company's biggest growth have come from difficult situations with other people. It is easy to be around people we like, but often there is as much, if not more, to be gained in understanding our own behaviors and beliefs by being around people we don't particularly like. If nothing else, it serves as a reminder of who we don't want to become.

I once knew a woman who controlled her environment perfectly. She didn't have people around who disagreed with her or challenged her or in any way rocked her boat. That way she was safe. If any of her friends did challenge her, they were kicked out of the group. Each time this happened, she would burn that bridge completely and there would be no reconciliation.

It worked from the standpoint of controlling what was in her immediate environment, but what she didn't realize was that there was a price to pay for this type of behavior. Her reputation suffered. People didn't want to work with her. People didn't want to invest in creating long-term relationships with her.

As a result, she began to feel badly about the way she had treated others, and she grew lonely and sad. In addition, she missed business opportunities to deepen relationships, was not given referrals, and couldn't continue to broaden her financial horizons. When you only keep people around who agree with you, you aren't challenged, and therefore you don't grow. Any vision or business that is not growing is stagnating, and will eventually end.

Not only do you never know where that person will resurface in your future, but you don't want someone damaging your reputation. So it is always best to leave everything on amicable terms. Be the sort of person that people bump into five years later and are genuinely excited and happy to see again.

Integrity—Be Truthful and Honest

To be persuasive, we must be believable.
To be believable, we must be credible.
To be credible, we must be truthful.

—Edward R. Murrow

Integrity is about adhering to a code of conduct. It is knowing the difference between right and wrong and sticking to that code no matter what. It's all very easy to stick to your principles when there is no pressure to do so, but what has singled out the outstanding men and women of history is that they have shown strength and determination in the face of opposition. Take Rosa Parks, for example. Her beliefs and ethics about right and wrong were so strong that she personally opposed segregation and, as a result, went down in history as a major force for change.

When Jesus of Nazareth invited prostitutes, tax collectors, and the poor to eat with him, he was demonstrating his integrity and beliefs in a way far more powerful than words alone could ever do. Despite being looked down upon by the church and the other religious leaders of the time, his actions communicated a very powerful message of inclusion and the love and acceptance of God for all. It was also a message of non-judgment and of loving one's neighbor. It was a great example of walking one's talk with congruency.

Don't, however, confuse honesty and integrity with the need to reveal all information. In *Harry Potter and the Sorcerer's Stone*, Harry's first adventure, toward the end of his journey, after he has defeated the Dark Lord, he asks Professor Dumbledore about his past and his parents.

> "Sir, there are some things I'd like to know, if you can tell me . . . things I want to know the truth about. . . "
>
> "The truth." Dumbledore sighed. "It is a beautiful and terrible thing, and should therefore be treated with great caution."

I happen to agree with him for a number of reasons. The first is that there is to some extent no such thing as *the* truth. There is only *a* truth. Secondly, there is such a thing as too much information. Why, for example, tell a client that you were up all night fixing a mistake that you made in preparation? It's the truth, but it doesn't help anyone. All it does is create doubt about your ability to do the job.

It's important, in communicating your intentions to the world, to sometimes hide your cards and keep a poker face. There have been times in my life when I felt the need to discuss all of my intentions with everyone. Honesty and integrity are two of my highest values, and I used to have a belief that to be absolutely honest, I would have to wear my intentions on my sleeve. The problem with that type of thinking is that it can often produce results that are not very satisfying. Revealing intentions is often detrimental to the end result. In a poker game, you would never show your hand to the other players. However, sometimes when we are trying to claim a strong position, we want to show the world our strength, reveal it to others, in order to build ourselves up.

I had a client call me not too long ago who was upset. He had set several goals in his business that he knew would stretch him. He considered the goals to be quite lofty, but he was resolved to make them happen. The reason he was upset was that his family didn't take him seriously, because he had let them down on a few occasions in the past. In an attempt to build himself up in their eyes, he told several of them about the new goals he had set—but they did not react enthusiastically. In fact, in his words they attempted to "beat him down" and convince him that he wasn't being realistic.

After I had talked with him for a while, I finally asked him, "How would your family members have felt if you had never said anything, but instead had simply come through with the results?"

"They would be very happy," he replied.

"And how would you feel if you had never said anything but had just shown up one day having produced the results?"

"Ecstatic," he replied.

His family wasn't attempting to hurt him; they were simply acting the only way they could based upon their beliefs about what was possible. They were doing the best they could with the resources they had available at the time. My client wanted to gain their respect by telling them what he had planned. This actually did just the opposite since they were only reminded of his past failures. The illusion was that he would get acceptance or power by revealing his intentions, when in fact it actually took them away. Moreover, if he did produce the result afterward, he would be proving them wrong and they might take less joy in his accomplishment. Often the best thing to do is to keep your hand to yourself like a master card player until the right moment comes to reveal your royal straight flush!

Don't Talk about "I"

They say the sweetest sound in any language is the sound of your own name. When communicating with others, you will find that most people are interested in themselves more than anything else. One effective way to increase your influence and effectiveness in communication is to stop speaking about yourself but instead engage others in discussion about themselves. Remember, in his 2000 State of the Union address, President Bill Clinton used the word *we* 208 times. This single small word goes a long way in establishing a strong team spirit.

Never Speak Poorly of Others

Speaking poorly of others is a surefire way to ruin your reputation. I worked with a man who spoke about everybody within the company behind their backs. He thought that he was gaining people's trust by confiding in them. What it actually did was show people that he couldn't be trusted and that he was liable to speak poorly about them, too, when they were not around. This practice also creates ill will and a lack of respect within a team, group, or organization.

One of my good friends, Jim, told me a story about an occasion when he was out to lunch with a prospective business associate. The woman he was having lunch with had had a few drinks and was beginning to get quite talkative. At one point in the luncheon, she overheard someone at a table next to them who had mentioned the name of someone who was a competitor in her line of work. When she overheard the name, she turned to the person who had mentioned it and said, "Oh, I know Mike!" The person sitting next to them asked, "How do you know Mike?" As they spoke, this woman revealed her opinion that "He's only out for himself and he rips people off all the time."

"Oh really," the other guy said. "What's your name?" She told him, and then he said, "Well, he's a good friend of mine. I'll let him know you feel that way."

It does us absolutely no good whatsoever to voice opinions like that, even if we believe they're true. It affects and tarnishes our reputations more then it does the person we are speaking of.

Stand Up for Your Beliefs

You can please some of the people all of the time and all of the people some of the time, but you can't please all of the people all of the time.
—Winston Churchill

The one trait that is consistent in almost every influential person I have ever researched or met is that they took a stand for what they believed in, no matter the consequences. They put their ideas or concepts out to the world despite the abuse or criticism that resulted. The moment you take a stand for anything, you will also encounter those in your world who oppose your position.

As Einstein once said, "Great spirits have always encountered violent opposition from mediocre minds." When Gandhi stood for the freedom of the Indian people, he was beaten down and thrown in jail by the British. When Nelson Mandela stood for the equality of the blacks in Africa, he was thrown in jail for a good portion of his life.

But because of their unwavering passion they won, and their contribution to their world has gone down in history. And who knows, yours may too!

CHAPTER

Conclusion: The One Thing That Can Change Everything

The measure of a man's real character is what he would do if he knew he never would be found out.
—Thomas B. Macaulay

One thing can change everything. One event, one thought, one act of kindness, one act of violence, one moment can change everything. Even this book could be your one thing that causes you to choose differently. Remember, it is not the events in our lives that determine our destiny, but what we decide about those events. Deciding to turn your dreams into realities and your passions into profits is the very first step in accomplishing just that.

We are each given our own individual universe to shape as we will. We are constantly shaping our universe all the time, either consciously or unconsciously. Every thought we have, every word we utter, every action we take communicates something to the universe around us and sculpts it in some way. By practicing and learning the skills taught in this book, you empower yourself to take conscious control of the tools that define your world each and every moment of your life. This book is not meant to be read one time through, but rather to be a reference and guidebook to be revisited over and over again.

Remember that you now have the power to strategically see, hear, feel, and create your future, then literally carve it out in the way you choose. You now have the power and knowledge to win the game of life in the way you want to see it play out.

The people who are able to produce the most in terms of results are those who have the ability to enlist the cooperation of others to assist them in accomplishing their objectives. By mastering your interpersonal communication skills as well as your ability to influence, you are empowered to produce extraordinary results.

You have the capacity to master all that is contained in this book. Use the tools to expand your rule book and reach outward with new strategies and skill sets to gain understanding and proficiency in new areas. Break through the boundary conditions of your current thinking to embrace *all* that is possible for you! By doing that you will forge opportunities you never thought possible and the playing field of your game will encompass so much more than you previously allowed. Figure 19.1 shows this expanded experience.

Most of all, learn to believe in yourself and your ability to create a magical reality—because reality is only what you choose it to be.

Always remember to use the strategies and techniques with heart

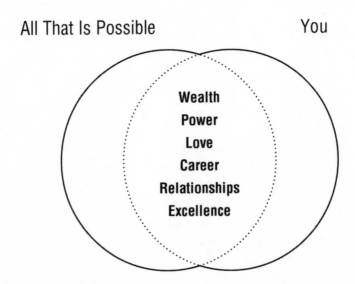

All That Is Possible **You**

Wealth

Power

Love

Career

Relationships

Excellence

Figure 19.1   An Expanded Playing Field in the Game of Life

and with caring for your brothers and sisters on the planet. Truly, if there is nothing outside of you and we are all one, then the golden rule becomes, "Do unto yourself as you would have done unto you." If people really understood that we are all one, the world would be a very different place. We would not harm others or our planet but instead live peacefully, respecting our differences, and caring for our natural resources.

When I was growing up, my grandparents had a small place on the beach near Ensenada, Mexico, that was always open—family and friends were welcome to stay there whenever they were in the area. My grandparents had only one request: that everyone who stayed there leave the place a little nicer than it was before they came. As you take these skills and go on your way to wealth, power, and influencing the world in positive ways, I have only one request: that you leave the world a little nicer than it was before you came. I hope to meet you at some point in the future. Until then, take care, dream big dreams, and make each day an extraordinary adventure.

Appendix: The Quantum Facts

*The "path" comes into existence
only when we observe it.*
—Werner Heisenberg, *Uncertainty Principle*

In 1927, physicist Werner Heisenberg set the cat among the pigeons by publishing *The Uncertainty Principle*. It had profound implications and started a debate about the very nature of reality that would rage the better part of 55 years.

Up until the time that science started to explore the quantum nature of the universe, it was popular to believe that the universe followed the laws of Newtonian Physics—that a "real world" existed independently of us, regardless of what we did in it. What Heisenberg's conclusive study on particle behavior did was blow that assumption apart. This had far-reaching implications from both a scientific and philosophical point of view.

Heisenberg's theory on particles states quite simply that "the more precisely the *position* is determined, the less precisely the *momentum* is known." Translated into classical physics, this meant that, contrary to popular belief, the future motion of a particle *could not* be exactly predicted, or determined, from a knowledge of its present position and momentum and all of the forces acting upon it.

In brief, Heisenberg's uncertainty principle implied that there was no concrete reality! Rather, reality depended on who or what was observing it.

Indeed, in quantum research, when scientists set up an experiment expecting light to behave as a wave, it behaved as a wave; when they presupposed it as a particle, it behaved as a particle. Many experiments in quantum physics have also told us that a quantum particle only exists as a possibility prior to our observing or measuring it; this means that *it doesn't exist until we look for it to exist.*

As you can imagine, in 1927, that was a pretty radical concept—and it still is today! The heavyweights of the time came out against it, Einstein being one of them. Einstein was perplexed that the simple act of observation could actually affect the object of observation. He did not believe that an observer could bring about drastic changes in the universe simply by looking at it.

Einstein believed that Heisenberg's interpretation of quantum mechanics was incomplete. So Einstein and a few buddies —Podoski and Rosen—set out to disprove Heisenberg's uncertainty principle in a thought experiment in 1935, known as the E.P.R. paradox.

In this thought experiment, these three leading quantum theorists postulated that one *could* know the position and momentum (or spin) of a quantum particle simultaneously, by sending two electrons out in separate directions from a single source pulse at the same speed and measuring the position of one and momentum of the other. Both position and momentum of each could be accurately predicted.

This led to a huge debate between Einstein and Niels Bohr, another leading quantum theorist who favored Heisenberg's ideas. Niels Bohr stated that Einstein's E.P.R. theory was based on the faulty assumption that observing the position of one didn't somehow affect the momentum of the other. Einstein claimed that it would be impossible for the observation of one electron to affect the other because that would mean that the electrons would have to communicate in some way across the quanta. And for that to occur, communication would have taken place at over seven times the speed of light, or instantaneously, which according to the theory of relativity was impossible. According to Einstein, nothing could move faster than the speed of light.

It wasn't until 1982 that the Einstein/Bohr debate was finally answered. In a laboratory at the University of Paris, a research team led by physicist Alain Aspect performed a series of experiments based upon a mathematical theorem that was put forward by John Bell in 1964, to settle the Einstein/Bohr debate. These experiments may turn out to be the most important experiments of the 20th century.

What has come to be known as the Aspect Experiment revealed something remarkable—that under certain circumstances, subatomic particles such as electrons are able to communicate with each other regardless of distance. This communication happened instantaneously, whether they were separated by a fraction of a millimeter or a hundred miles. According to Einstein, it wasn't possible because it meant that the communication traveled faster than anything, even light, which at the time was considered impossible. Aspect, however, in 1982, proved once and for all that not only did they communicate but they did so instantaneously—what one particle knew, they all knew at the same time.

The Aspect experiment implied that there is an underlying connectedness to everything in the universe. However, this same experiment proved something else as well. It proved what Heisenberg had stated in his *Uncertainty Principle*, that *in a quantum reality, the observer always and intimately affects the observed*. In fact, you can't observe something *without* affecting it.

And here's where it starts to get really interesting . . . .

In the University of London, physicist David Bohm took Aspect's findings one step further and suggested that objective reality does not exist at all and that, despite an apparent solidity, the universe is essentially an illusion—a gigantic, intricately detailed, and complex holographic illusion.

To understand why Bohm makes such a startling assertion, it is important to explain what a hologram is. A hologram is a three-dimensional image made with the aid of a laser. If you are a Star Trek fan, you will be aware of holograms and the holodeck (which, as we will see, may be closer to reality than we would have ever thought possible.) Or perhaps you saw a hologram used in *Star Wars*, when R2D2 projects a 3-D image of Princess Leia bearing a message from Obi-Wan Kenobi.

To make a hologram, the object is first cast in the light of a laser beam. Then a second laser beam is bounced off the reflected light of the first. The point where they meet is captured on film. When the film is developed it looks like a meaningless swirl of light and dark lines. But as soon as the developed film is illuminated by another laser beam, a three-dimensional image of the original object appears.

What is so fascinating is that if you create a hologram of an apple and then you cut the holographic image in half—or, for that matter, into a thousand pieces—each piece will contain the whole image of the apple, just a smaller but complete version of it. Each part of a hologram therefore contains all the information possessed by the whole. The whole is in every part. This could explain why communication between particles is instantaneous—the universe is holographic in nature, and therefore everything in it is a part of the whole. The particles are not necessarily communicating but, rather, their separateness is just an illusion. They are part of the whole, and the whole is in the part. Bohm argues that at some deeper level of reality, such particles are not individual entities but are actually extensions of the same fundamental whole.

To enable people to better understand this idea, Bohm offers the following example. Imagine an aquarium. You are watching all the action by way of closed circuit TV. There are two screens relating to two cameras trained on the aquarium from two difference angles. As you watch the two screens, you might assume that you are actually watching two different aquariums. You continue to watch and start to notice that when one fish moves, the fish on the other screen makes a corresponding change. Amazing, you think—these fish must be communicating with each other.

This, says Bohm, is precisely what is going on between the subatomic particles in Aspect's experiment. According to Bohm, the apparent faster-than-light connection is really telling us that there is some deeper level of reality we are not privy to, a more complex dimension. In the aquarium example where there were not two fish at all—just one fish seen from different perspectives. We were simply not able to see the full picture to be able to work that out.

In addition to the mind-bending qualities you may currently be experiencing, such a holographic universe would possess other amazing features. If separateness is an illusion, it means that at some level we do not yet understand, we are all interconnected. We are all just swimming in a quantum ocean of pure potentiality. Modern science is now restating what the ancient traditions have always held to be true—that you are one with everything in the universe. Everything is one energy manifesting in almost infinite diversity. As scientists began to study more and more minute levels of matter, they began to see that at the smallest levels—smaller than the atom—there is more space than there is solidity. In fact, if you examined this book, or yourself for that matter, under a high-powered microscope you would see more space than you would solid matter. According to quantum field theorists, the atoms of which the book is made are 99.999 percent composed of the void and emptiness of space. The subatomic particles are impulses of energy and information. What gives the appearance of matter is the arrangement and quantity of the subatomic particles. The density of the arrangement and the vibratory rate determine the form that something takes in the material world.

So a BMW, a pitbull terrier, you, the Grand Canyon, Niagara Falls, and the Sydney Opera House—everything in the world right now is made up of exactly the same stuff. Look around you right now. Everything you can see and touch is the same matter—every person, every object, and every star in the sky. The only thing that is different about each thing is the density and vibrational frequency.

Bohm is not the only researcher who has found evidence that the universe is a hologram. Working independently in the field of brain research, Stanford neurophysiologist Karl Pribram has also realized the holographic nature of reality.

Pribram was drawn to the holographic model by the puzzle of how and where memories are stored in the brain. For decades, numerous studies have shown that rather than being confined to a specific location, memories are dispersed throughout the brain.

Beginning in 1913, Canadian neurosurgeon Wilder Penfield did several experiments in which he probed his patients' brains with an electrode in an attempt to cure their epilepsy. In the 1930s, he made some astounding discoveries. In one case, he found while studying a female patient that when he touched certain areas of her brain, she recalled a vivid memory of being in her kitchen and hearing the sounds of her little boy playing outside. She could also hear the sounds of the passing automobiles and other neighborhood noises.

What Penfield had actually discovered was that the stimulation of a certain portion of the cerebral cortex could evoke incredibly vivid memories. Penfield's research led many scientists at the time to believe that *memory* was stored *in* the brain. This belief about the storage of memory was widely held in the scientific community for many years, although it remained impossible to find the *individual* locations of *specific* memories.

In a series of landmark experiments in the 1920s, brain scientist Karl Lashley found that no matter what portion of a rat's brain he removed, the rat was still able to run a complex maze it had been taught prior to surgery. In fact, when the rat was left with nothing but a brain stem it was still able to run the maze.

It was in the late 1950s that Karl Pribram, a leading neurophysiologist from Stanford University, took up the case and proposed his groundbreaking theory for the *holographic* storage of memory. He explained that in Karl Lashley's experiments it was possible for the rats to continue to run the maze even without much of a brain, because the memory was not in a specific location in the brain but, rather, was stored holographically throughout the entire brain.

Pribram believes memories are encoded not in neurons or small groupings of neurons, but in patterns of nerve impulses that crisscross the entire brain in the same way that patterns of laser light crisscross the entire area of a piece of film containing a holographic image. In other words, Pribram believes the brain itself is a hologram.

Pribram's theory also explains how the human brain can store so many memories in so little space. It has been estimated that the human brain has the capacity to memorize something on the order of 10 billion bits of information during the average human lifetime (or roughly the same amount of information contained in five sets of the *Encyclopedia Britannica*).

The storage of memory is not the only neurophysiological puzzle that becomes more feasible in light of Pribram's holographic model of the brain. Another is how the brain is able to translate the avalanche of frequencies it receives via the senses into the concrete world of our perceptions. Encoding and decoding frequencies is precisely what a hologram does best. Pribram concludes that, just as a hologram functions as a sort of lens—a translating device able to convert an apparently meaningless blur of frequencies into a coherent image—the brain also comprises a lens and uses holographic principles to convert the frequencies it receives through the senses into hard reality.

But the most mind-boggling aspect of Pribram's holographic model of the brain is what happens when it is put together with Bohm's theory. For if the concreteness of the world is but a secondary reality and what is "there" is actually a holographic blur of frequencies, and if the brain is also a hologram and only selects some of the frequencies out of this blur and transforms them into sensory perceptions, what becomes of objective reality?

Put quite simply, it ceases to exist. As the religions of the East have long upheld, the material world is maya, an illusion, and although we may think we are physical beings moving through a physical world, this, too, is an illusion. We are like receivers floating through a kaleidoscopic sea of frequency, and what we extract from this sea and interpret into physical reality is but one view taken from an infinite sea of possibility. The implications of this perspective are enormous.

Just think about it for a second. If reality is different for everyone because everyone translates frequency differently, and therefore everyone chooses a different experience from a sea of possibility, doesn't it then follow that if you can understand more about the way you translate the frequency, you then have the power to change your world? So if you don't particularly enjoy your current reality, you have the opportunity to shift your focus to an alternative reality from the sea of possibilities.

The implications are indeed profound. If it is all just a hologram with an infinite number of possible channels to choose from, and all we need to do is tune in to whatever we choose to experience, then there truly are no limits to the extent to which you can alter the fabric and outcomes of your life. All things exist in this quantum soup of pure potentiality. Your external reality is nothing but a blank canvas, on which to create your masterpiece.

Bibliography

Ansari, Masud. *Modern Hypnosis.* Washington, DC: Mas-Press, 1982.

Arabian Knights. Babelserg, Germany: Babelsberg International Film Produktion, Hallmark Entertainment, 1999.

Bandler, Richard, and John La Valle. *Persuasion Engineering.* Capitola, CA: Meta Publications, Inc., 1966.

Beckwith, Michael. *40 Day Mind Fast Soul Feast.* Culver City, CA: Agape Publishing, Inc., 2000.

Birdwhistell, Ray L. *Kinesics and Context.* Philadelphia: University of Pennsylvania Press, 1970.

Bower, Tom. *Branson.* London: HarperCollins, 2000.

Branson, Richard. *Losing My Virginity: Richard Branson—The Autobiography.* Sydney, Australia: Random House, 1999.

Brown, Mick. *Richard Branson: The Authorised Biography.* London: Headline Book Publishing, 1988.

Buffett, Mary, and David Clark. *The New Buffettology.* London: Simon & Schuster Ltd., 2002.

Buffett, Warren, and Lawrence A. Cunningham. *The Essays of Warren Buffett: Lessons for Corporate America.* Newton, MA: The Cunningham Group, 2001. 1997.

Buzan, Tony, with Barry Buzan. *The Mind Map Book: How to Use Radiant Thinking to Maximize Your Brain's Untapped Potential.* New York: Penguin Books, 1993.

Carnegie, Dale. *Lifetime Plan for Success.* New York: Galahad Books, 1998.

Carroll, Lewis. *Alice in Wonderland.* New York: W.W. Norton & Company, 1971.

Chopra, Deepak. *Ageless Body, Timeless Mind.* New York: Harmony Books, 1993.

———. *Creating Affluence: Wealth Consciousness in the Field of All Possibilities.* San Rafael, CA: New World Library, 1993.

———. *Quantum Healing.* New York: Bantam Books, 1989.

Cialdini, Robert B. *Influence: The Psychology of Persuasion.* New York: Quill, 1984.

Csikszentmihalyi, Mihaly. *Flow: The Psychology of Optimal Experience.* New York: Harper & Row Publishers, 1990.

Dearlove, Des. *Business the Richard Branson Way: 10 Secrets of the World's Greatest Brand Builder.* New York: AMACOM, 1999.

Dilts, Robert. *Sleight of Mouth.* Capitola, CA: Meta Publications, 1999.

Frankl, Viktor. *Man's Search for Meaning.* Boston: Beacon Press, 2000.

Fridson, Martin S. *How to Be a Billionaire: Proven Strategies from the Titans of Wealth.* New York: John Wiley & Sons, Inc., 2000.

Gaines, Charles. "Staying Hungry." *Men's Health Magazine,* 2004.

Gleick, James. *Chaos: Making a New Science.* New York: Viking Press, 1987.

Goodwin, Paul A. *Foundation Theory: Report on the Efficacy of the Formal Education Process in Rural Alaska.* Volume I, *Advanced Neuro Dynamics.* Honolulu: 1988.

Gordon, David, and Maribeth Meyers-Anderson. *Phoenix.* Capitola, CA: Meta Publications, 1981.

Graham, Benjamin. *The Intelligent Investor: The Definitive Book of Value Investing.* New York: HarperCollins, 1984.

The Great Outdoors. Los Angeles: Universal Studios, 1988.

The Greatest Speeches of All Time. Rolling Bay, WA: The Nostalgia Company, 1998.

Greene, Robert. *The 48 Laws of Power.* New York: Viking Penguin, 1998.

Griffith, Joe. *Speaker's Library of Business Quotations.* Englewood Cliffs, NJ: Prentice Hall, 1990.

Hart, Michael H. *The 100: A Ranking of the Most Influential Persons in History.* New York: Hart Publishing Company, 1978.

Hawking, Stephen. *The Universe in a Nutshell*. New York: Bantam Books, 2001.

Hill, Napoleon. *Think and Grow Rich*. New York: Ballantine Books, 1976.

Jackson, Tim. *Virgin King: Inside Richard Branson's Business Empire*. London: HarperCollins, 1994.

Jung, Carl G. *Man and His Symbols*. New York: Doubleday, 1964.

Jung, Carl, G. Adler, and R.F.C. Hull. *Psychological Types*. Princeton, NJ: Princeton University Press, 1971.

Karrass, Chester L. *The Negotiating Game*. New York: Harper Business, 1992.

———. *In Business as in Life—You Don't Get What You Deserve, You Get What You Negotiate*. Beverly Hills, CA: Stanford St. Press, 1996.

Katherine, Anne. *Boundaries*. New York: Parkside Publishing Corporation, 1991.

Knight, Sue. *NLP at Work: The Difference That Makes a Difference in Business*. London: Nicholas Brealey Publishing, 1995.

Korzybski, Alfred. *Science and Sanity: An Introduction to Non-Aristotelian Systems and General Semantics*. Brooklyn, NY: Institute of General Semantics, 1995.

Krasner, A.M. *The Wizard Within*. Irvine, CA: American Board of Hypnotherapy Press, 1990–1991.

Laborde, Genie Z. *Influencing with Integrity: Management Skills for Communication and Negotiation*. Palo Alto, CA: Syntony Publishing, 1983.

The Long Walk of Nelson Mandela. New York: UnaPix Entertainment, Inc., and WGBH/Frontline, 1999.

Lowe, Janet. *Warren Buffett Speaks: Wit and Wisdom from the World's Greatest Investor*. New York: John Wiley & Sons, 1997.

———. *Ted Turner Speaks: Insights from the World's Greatest Maverick*. New York: John Wiley & Sons, 1999.

Lowenstein, Roger. *Buffett: The Making of an American Capitalist*. New York: Doubleday, 1995.

Martin Luther King Jr., The Man and the Dream. New York: New Video Group, 1997.

Massey, Morris. *The People Puzzle*. Reston, VA: Reston Publishing Company, 1979.

McCrone, John. *Essential Science: How the Brain Works*. New York: DK Publishing, 2002.

Myss, Caroline. *Anatomy of the Spirit*. New York: Three Rivers Press, 1996.

Neisser, Ulric. *Cognition and Reality*. New York: W.H. Freeman Company, 1981.

Penfield, Wilder. *The Mystery of the Mind: A Critical Study of Consciousness and the Human Brain*. Princeton, NJ: Princeton University Press, 1975.

Peters, Thomas J., and Robert H. Waterman Jr. *In Search of Excellence*. New York: Harper & Row Publishers, 1982.

Ponder, Catherine. *The Dynamic Laws of Prosperity*. Marina del Rey, CA: DeVorss & Company, 1962.

Ries, Al, and Jack Trout. *Positioning*. New York: Warner Books, 1981.

Robbins, Anthony. *Unlimited Power*. New York: Simon & Schuster, 1986.

Rohm, Wendy Goldman. *The Murdoch Mission*. New York: John Wiley & Sons, 2002.

Rohmann, Chris. *A World of Ideas*. New York: Ballantine Publishing Group, 1999.

Rowling, J.K. *Harry Potter and the Sorcerer's Stone*. New York: Scholastic, 1997.

Satir, Virginia. *The New Peoplemaking*. Mountain View, CA: Science and Behavior Books, Inc., 1988.

Sharp, Daryl. *C.G. Jung Lexicon*. Toronto: Inner City Books, 1991.

Shawcross, William. *Murdoch: The Making of a Media Empire*. New York: Simon & Schuster Touchstone, 2002.

Talbot, Michael. *The Holographic Universe*. New York: HarperCollins, 1991.

Trump, Donald J., with Tony Schwartz. *Trump: The Art of the Deal*. New York: Warner Books, 1987.

Walsch, Neale Donald. *The Little Soul and the Sun*. Charlottesville, VA: Hampton Roads Publishing Company, 1998.

Wolf, Fred Alan. *Taking the Quantum Leap*. New York: Harper & Row Publishers, 1981.

Christopher Howard's Seminars and Trainings

University of Excellence

Breakthrough to Success—Wealth and Power Weekend™
It's within this two-and-a-half-day life-changing event that you finally release anything holding you back in life, then use Strategic Visioning™ to create the future you ultimately desire.

Performance Revolution
Master persuasive communication in this exciting weekend with win-win sales and negotiating. Take your finances or business to a whole new level with the basics of Cognitive Reimprinting™.

Billionaire Bootcamp
After installing your role models' success strategies with Cognitive Reimprinting™, this one-week intensive event gives you the ability to inspire others toward the fulfillment of your unique vision.

Design Your Destiny
In this three-and-a-half-day experience you will get clear on your passion and purpose is in life, plot your course, then begin to take powerful steps to create your ultimate destiny.

Leadership and Coaching Academy

Results Coach Certification
This one-week training gives you leading-edge tools to coach yourself and others to break through behavioral patterns and produce exceptional results in any area. Launch a new career or augment your current one with this professional certification training.

Master Results Coach and Performance Consultant Certification
Get the full range of accelerated human change techniques. Coach, consult, and empower people, businesses, and organizations to achieve optimal and consistent performance.

Professional Speaker and Platform Skills Training
In this one-week training, you vastly expand your personal and professional sphere of influence. Install 36 behaviors of the most effective speakers and learn to connect a crowd from the stage.

Available Products

Performance Revolution (8-CD set)
Gain the business strategies that multiply returns—how to create a team, negotiate win-win situations, and consistently hit your goals.

Stepping into Wealth (3-CD set)
Change your perceptions to instantly transform your financial destiny. Includes a powerful hypnotic induction to erase limiting beliefs and install a wealthy mindset at ever-deeper levels.

Skyrocket Your Sales (2-CD set)
Master the skills of persuasive language to increase your sales, close deals, generate prospects, and respond to objections. Includes hypnotic induction to achieve your specific, financial goals.

The 7 Keys to Wealth (2-CD set)
Learn from multibillionaires the seven behaviors and beliefs that consistently generate wealth, then unlearn the misconceptions and bad money habits that rob you of opportunities to prosper.

Index

About the Author

Christopher Howard
Entrepreneur, Leadership Advisor, and Master Results Trainer

Christopher Howard is one of the world's leading authorities on the psychology of wealth and accelerated personal achievement. As an entrepreneur and CEO of The Christopher Howard Companies, he has developed a system to replicate the success strategies of the world's most legendary leaders and billionaires that has assisted tens of thousands of individuals and businesses worldwide to achieve long-lasting, breakthrough performance results. His dynamic presence and unique approach to attaining wealth and fulfillment captivate growing audiences each year through public seminars, television, and radio. Chris' clients include politicians, Fortune 500 executives, celebrities, and thousands of people from all walks of life who want to live their ultimate vision for their lives.